英汉对照·心灵阅读（二）

Life

生活篇

张斌彦 董新颖　编译

林　立　　　审校

外文出版社

卷首语

总有一种感动无处不在。

总有一种情怀轻舞飞扬。

总有一种生活,在别处,闪动异样的光芒。

阅读,让我们的生活在情调与知性中享受更多……

故事与见闻,犹如生活的魅力与智慧,合着我们自身生命的光与影,陪伴我们一路前行。

快乐和圆满,幻想与失落,飞扬的眼泪,

行走江湖的落拓，不与人说的痛苦，渐行渐远的繁华，坚持的勇气，点点滴滴的小意思……

人生让我们感受到的，也许远远不只是这些；更多的是挫折后生长的力量，沉闷时的豁然开朗，是屋前那静静的南山上盛开的人淡如菊的境界，是闹市中跋涉红尘、豪情万丈的冲动，是很纯粹的一杯午后的香醇的咖啡……

漫步红尘，有彻悟来自他人的故事，有灵犀来自偶然的相遇，在这里，一种从未见过的却可能早就在我们心底的生活方式有可能与我们邂逅。

让我们一起阅读吧，感受生长的智慧、风雅与力量。

Contents
目 录

Puppies for sale

出售小狗

I don't run too well myself, and he will need someone who understands.

我自己也跑不好，它需要有个理解它的人。

A farmer had some puppies[1] he needed to sell. He painted a sign advertising[2] the pups and set about nailing it to a post on the edge of his yard. As he was driving the last nail into the post, he felt a tug on his overalls. He looked down into the Eyes of a little boy.

"Mister," he said, "I want to buy one of your puppies."

"Well,"said the farmer, as he rubbed the sweat[3] off the back of his neck, "these puppies come from fine parents and cost a good deal of money."

The boy dropped his head for a moment. Then reaching deep into his pocket, he pulled out a handful of change and held it up to the farmer. "I've got thirty-nine cents. Is that enough to take a look? "

"Sure," said the farmer.

And with that he let out a whistle[4], "Here, Dolly! " he called.

Out from the doghouse and down the ramp ran Dolly followed by four little balls of fur. The little boy pressed his face against the chain link fence. His eyes danced with delight. As the dogs made their way to the fence, the little boy noticed something else stirring[5] inside the doghouse. Slowly another little ball appeared; This one noticeably smaller. Down the ramp it slid. Then in a somewhat awkward manner the little pup began hobbling to

一个农夫有几只小狗需要出售。他用漆刷了一张售小狗的广告牌，然后着手把牌子钉在他家院子旁边的柱子上。当他钉到最后一个钉子时，他感到有人拉他的外罩。他低头看见一双小孩的眼睛。

"先生，"他说："我想买你一只小狗。"

"嗯，"农夫一边擦着脖子后的汗水一边说："这些小狗血统高贵，值很多钱。"

男孩低头想了一会儿，然后把手伸到口袋深处拿出一把零钱递给了农夫说："我有39美分。这钱够不够看上一眼？"

"当然可以。"农夫说。

同意之后农夫吹了一声口哨："过来，多利。"他喊道。多利顺着小道从狗棚里跑了出来，身后跟着四个毛茸茸的小球。小男孩的脸紧紧地贴在一排篱笆墙上，眼里充满了欣喜。当小狗们跑向篱笆时，小男孩注意到狗棚里有些异样，只见又一只毛茸茸的小球出现了，这只小狗看上去明显就比其它小狗瘦小。他顺着小道滑了下来。然后他开始笨拙地去追其他小狗，想尽力赶上它们……

"我想要这只小狗，"小男孩指着这只小狗说。

农夫蹲在小男孩身边说："孩子，你不会

❶ puppies
/ˈpʌpɪz/
n. pl. 小狗

❷ advertise
/ˈædvətaɪz/
v. 为...做广告

❸ sweat /swet/
n. 汗水

❹ whistle /ˈwɪsl/
n. 口哨声

❺ stirring
/ˈstɜːrɪŋ/
adj. 热闹的

ward the others, doing its best to catch up....

"I want that one," the little boy said, pointing to the runt.

· The farmer knelt down at the boy's side and said, "Son, you don't want that puppy. He will never be able to run and play with you like these other dogs would."

With that the little boy stepped back from the fence, reached down, and began rolling up one leg of his trousers. In doing so he revealed a steel brace[6] running down both sides of his leg attaching itself to a specially made shoe. Looking back up at the farmer, he said, "You see sir, I don't run too well myself, and he will need *someone* who understands."

The world is full of people who need someone who understands.

想要那只小狗的。它永远跑不动，不会像其他小狗一样陪你玩儿。"

　　听到农夫这样说，小男孩离开篱笆墙低头开始卷自己的裤腿。只见他的腿两边夹着一幅铁制支架。固定在一只特制的鞋上。他抬头看着农夫说："先生，你看，我自己也跑不好，它需要有个理解它的人。"

　　这个世界充满了需要理解的人。

❻ brace

/breɪs/

n. 支柱

Parable[1] of the pencil

铅笔的寓言

Never allow yourself to get discouraged and think that your life is insignificant and cannot make a change.

永远别让自己灰心，不要认为自己的生活毫无意义并且无法改变。

The Pencil Maker took the pencil aside, just before putting him into the box.

"There are 5 things you need to know," he told the pencil, "Before I send you out into the world. Always remember them and never forget, and you will become the best pencil you can be.

"One: You will be able to do many great things, but only if you allow yourself to be held in *someone's* hand.

"Two: You will experience a painful[2] sharpening[3] from time to time, but you'll need it to become a better pencil.

"Three: You will be able to correct any mistakes you might make.

"Four: The most important part of you will always be what's inside.

"And Five: On every surface[4] you are used on, you must leave your mark. No matter what the condition, you must continue to write."

The pencil understood and promised to remember, and went into the box with purpose in its heart.

Now replacing the place of the pencil with you. Always remember them and never forget, and you will become the best

铅笔制造商在把铅笔放回铅笔盒里之前，先把它拿到了一边。

"你需要知道五件事情，"他告诉铅笔说，"在我把你送到这世界之前，要一直记住这五件事，永远不要忘记，这样就可以尽你所能成为最好的铅笔。

"一、你将能够做出许多伟大的事情来，但条件是你必须允许自己被握在别人的手中。

"二、你将会经历一次又一次被削得锋利的痛苦，但是你需要这样的经历来使你为更好的铅笔。

"三、你将要改正你可能干过的任何错误。

"四、你身上最重要的部分是你的内心。

"还有五，在你被使用的每一个表面上，你都要留下标记。不管在什么样的情况下，你都要继续写下去。"

铅笔听明白了，它答应会永远记住这些话的。然后心里带着这目标进了盒子。

现在把你的位置和铅笔换一换。要一直记住，永远不要忘记这些话。你就会尽你所能成为出色的人。

一、你能够做出很多伟大的事，但是你要把自己交给上帝，允许别人因为你拥有的天赋而去接受你。

二、你将会因为经历生活中的各种问题

---

❶ **parable**
/ˈpærəbl/
n. 道德小故事
❷ **painful**
/ˈpeɪnfl/
adj. 痛苦的
❸ **sharpen**
/ˈʃɑːpən/
v. 削尖
❹ **surface**
/ˈsɜːfɪs/
n. 表面

person you can be.

One: You will be able to do many great things, but only if you allow yourself to be held in God's hand. And allow other human beings to access you for the many gifts you possess[5].

Two: You will experience a painful sharpening from time to time, by going through various problems in life, but you'll need it to become a stronger person.

Three: You will be able to correct any mistakes you might make.

Four: The most important part of you will always be what's on the inside.

And Five: On every surface you walk through, you must leave your mark. No matter what the situation, you must continue to do your duties.

Allow this parable on the pencil to encourage you to know that you are a special person and only you can fulfill the purpose to which you were born to accomplish.

Never allow yourself to get discouraged and think that your life is insignificant[6] and cannot make a change.

而体验一次又一次被打磨的痛苦，但是你需要这样的痛苦而使你成为更坚强的人。

三、你将能够纠正你可能犯的任何错误。

四、你身上最重要的部分是你的内在品质。

五、在你所走过的每个路面上，你必须留下你的足迹。无论在什么样的境况下，你都要继续尽你的职责。

让这个关于铅笔的寓言故事激励你并使你知道你是特殊的，而且只有你自己才可以完成你与生俱来的目标。

永远别让自己灰心，不要认为自己的生活毫无意义并且无法改变。

❺ **possess**
/pəˈzes/
v. 拥有

❻ **insignificant**
/ˌɪnsɪgˈnɪfɪkənt/
adj. 无意义的

The man in the moon
月亮上的人

I no longer want to cut stone. I would be the sun; that would be pleasant.

我不想砍伐石头了。我想做太阳，那一定非常有意思。

There was a blacksmith[1] once who complained[2]: "I am not well, and my work is too warm. I want to be a stone on the mountain. There it must be cool, for the wind blows and the trees give a shade[3]." A wise man who had power over all things replied: "Go you, be a stone." And he was a stone, high up on the mountainside. It happened that a stonecutter came that way for a stone, and when he saw the one that had been the blacksmith, he knew that it was what he sought, and he began to cut it. The stone cried out: "This hurts! I no longer want to be a stone. A stonecutter I want to be. That would be pleasant." The wise man, humoring[4] him, said, "Be a cutter." Thus he became a stone-cutter, and as he went seeking suitable[5] stone, he grew tired, and his feet were sore. He whimpered, " I no longer want to cut stone. I would be the sun; that would be pleasant." The wise man commanded, " Be the sun." And he was the sun. But the sun was warmer than the blacksmith, than a stone, than a stonecutter, and he complained, "I do not like this. I would be the moon. It looks cool." The wise man spoke yet again, "Be the moon." And he was the moon. "This is warmer than being the sun," murmured he, "for the light from the sun shines on me ever. I do not want to be the moon. I would be a smith again. That, verily[6], is the best life." But the wise man replied, " I am weary of your changing. You wanted to be the moon; the moon you are, and it you will remain."

And in yon high heaven lives he to this day.

有个铁匠一次抱怨说："我过得不好，我的工作太热了。我想做块山上的石头。那里一定非常凉快，因为那里有风吹拂，有树遮荫。"一位掌管万物的智者回答："去吧，做个石头。"于是他就成了高处山边的一块石头。碰巧一个石匠来到这里找一块石头。当他看见那块曾经是铁匠的石头，他知道那就是他要找的那块石头。

于是他开始砍伐，石头叫喊道："弄疼我了，我不想再做石头了。我想做石匠，那一定非常有意思。"智者迁就了他。说："做个石匠吧。"这样他变成了一个石匠。当他去寻找合适的石头时，他累了，脚直发酸。他抱怨道："我不想砍伐石头了。我想做太阳。那一定非常有意思。"智者命令道："做个太阳吧。"然后他变成了太阳。但是太阳又比作铁匠、石头、石匠热。他于是抱怨道："我不喜欢做太阳，我想做月亮。它看上去非常凉爽。"智者又说："做月亮去吧。"于是他变成了月亮。"这个要比做太阳还热呢，"他嘟囔着说，"因为太阳光总照着我。我不想做月亮了。我还是想再做铁匠。实际上那的确是最好的生活。"但是智者回答说："你变来变去，我都累了。你想做月亮，就去做月亮吧。永远都不再变了。"

于是他在那月亮上一直生活至今。

❶ **blacksmith**

/ˈblæksmɪθ/

n. 石匠

❷ **complain**

/ˈkɒmpleɪn/

v. 埋怨，抱怨

❸ **shade**

/ʃeɪd/

n. 阴凉

❹ **humor**

/ˈhjuːmə/

n./v. 应和；迁就

❺ **suitable**

/ˈsjuːtəbl/

adj. 合适的

❻ **verily**

/ˈverɪlɪ/

adv. (古)确实地

Allow your own inner light to guide you

让内心的灯指引你

Work hard at what you like to do and try to overcome all obstacles.

做自己喜欢做的事，克服重重困难，不畏艰难险阻。

There comes a time when you must stand alone.

You must feel confident[1] enough within yourself to follow your own dreams.

You must be willing to make sacrifices[2].

You must be capable of changing and rearranging your priorities[3], so that your final goal can be achieved.

Sometimes, familiarity[4] and comfort need to be challenged.

There are times when you must take a few extra chances and create your own realities.

Be strong enough to at least try to make your life better.

Be confident enough that you won't settle for a compromise[5] just to get by.

Appreciate yourself by allowing yourself the opportunities[6] to grow, develop, and find your true sense of purpose in this life.

Don't stand in someone else's shadow when it's your sunlight that should lead the way.

Work hard at what you like to do and try to overcome all obstacles.

Laugh at your mistakes and praise yourself for learning from them.

Pick some flowers and appreciate the beauty of nature.

Say hello to strangers and enjoy the people you know.

Don't be afraid to show your emotions, laughing and crying make you feel better.

Love your friends and family with your entire being they are the most important part of your life.

Feel the calmness on a quiet sunny day.

Find a rainbow and live your world of dreams, always remember life is better than it seems.

当你必须一个人独自停留，

你要足够自信，坚定地追寻自己的梦，

并必须愿意为之付出。

你必须能够改变自我，决定孰轻孰重，重新

安排自己的生活，才能达到成功的彼岸。

有时候你需要挑战熟悉与安逸，

抓住更多的机会，创造属于自己的未来。

你需要足够坚强，至少要为美好生活作出努力。

相信自己，不要妥协，不要得过且过。

你需要学会欣赏自己，主动寻找机会，发现

生活的真正意义。

不要生活在别人的阴影里，让自己的阳光指

引自己。

做自己喜欢做的事，克服重重困难，不畏艰

难险阻。

嘲笑自己的错误，表扬自己的优点，因为你

会从错误中学习。

摘几朵花，享受大自然的美丽。

向陌生人打招呼，同熟人聊天。

不要害怕展示自己的内心世界，想哭就哭，

想笑就笑，感觉会更好。

用全心去爱自己的朋友家人，他们是你生活

中最重要的部分。

在阳光明媚的日子里，感受宁静。

寻一轮七彩虹，追求自己的梦想世界，永远

铭记生活要比看上去更美。

❶ confident
/ˈkɒnfɪdənt/
adj. 自信的

❷ sacrifice
/ˈsækrɪfaɪs/
n. 牺牲

❸ priority
/praɪˈɒrətɪ/
n. 优先；优先考虑
的事

❹ familiarity
/fəˌmɪlɪˈærətɪ/
n. 熟悉；亲密

❺ compromise
/ˈkɒmprəmaɪz/
n. 和解；让步

❻ opportunity
/ˌɒpəˈtjuːnətɪ/
n. 机会

Building your house
建造你的房子

This is your house... my gift to you.

这是你的房子，这是我送给你的礼物

An elderly carpenter[1] was ready to retire. He told his employer-contractor of his plans to leave the house-building business to live a more leisurely life with his wife and enjoy his extended[2] family. He would miss the paycheck each week, but he wanted to retire. They could get by.

The contractor was sorry to see his good worker go & asked if he could build just one more house as a personal favor. The carpenter said yes, but over time it was easy to see that his heart was not in his work. He resorted to shoddy workmanship[3] and used inferior[4] materials. It was an unfortunate way to end a dedicated[5] career.

When the carpenter finished his work, his employer came to inspect the house. Then he handed the front-door key to the carpenter and said, "This is your house... my gift to you."

The carpenter was shocked!

What a shame! If he had only known he was building his own house, he would have done it all so differently.

So it is with us. We build our lives, a day at a time, often putting less than our best into the building. Then, with a shock, we realize we have to live in the house we have built. If we could do it over, we would do it much differently.

But, you cannot go back. You are the carpenter, and every

一位年老的木匠准备退休，就告诉他的合同雇主，他计划放下建房子的生意，和他的妻子过一种更加悠闲的生活，并享受大家庭的天伦之乐，虽然他将会因此失去周薪，但是他还是想退休。他们可以这样生活。

雇主看见自己的好工人要离去感到很遗憾，就问他是否可以再建一座房子，就当是他的个人爱好。木匠答应了，但是过了一段时间后，大家很容易就发现他的心思不在工作上，他手艺粗糙，使用劣质的建筑材料，就这样老木匠为自己的木匠生涯画上了一个不圆满的句号。

房子建成后，合同雇主来检查房子的建筑质量，雇主把房子的前门钥匙交给木匠并说："这是你的房子，这是我送给你的礼物"。

木匠惊呆了！

天哪！如果他早知道他是给自己建房子，他一定不会偷工减料的。

有时在生活中我们也会犯同样的错误，一天之间我们就建成了自己的生活之屋，当然我们不会尽最大努力去建造它，当后来发现我们不得不居住在自己搭造的生活之屋中，我们同样感到愕然，如果一切可以重新再来，我们一定会认真对待的。

但是世上没有卖后悔药的，你就像是那

❶ **carpenter**
/ˈkɑːpəntə/
n. 木匠

❷ **extended**
/ɪkˈstendɪd/
adj. 扩大的

❸ **workmanship**
/ˈwɜːkmənˌʃɪp/
n. 手艺，技巧

❹ **inferior**
/ɪnˈfɪərɪə/
adj. 较低的

❺ **dedicated**
/ˈdedɪkeɪtɪd/
adj. 献身的；奉献一生的

❻ **erect** /ɪˈrekt/
v. 建造

day you hammer a nail, place a board, or erect[6] a wall. Someone once said, "Life is a do-it-yourself project." Your attitude and the choices you make today helps build the "house" you will live in tomorrow. Therefore, build wisely!

个木匠，每天，你钉个钉子，置块木板，砌堵墙。有人曾经说："生活是自己动手的工程"。你的心态和今天所做的选择决定着你明天所居住房子的质量。因此认认真真地建造它吧！

A lesson in life

生活的课堂

You can make of your life anything you wish.
Create your own life and then go out and live.

你可以按照你所期望的那样创造你自己的生活，活出自我。

Everything happens for a reason. Nothing happens by chance or by means of good or bad luck. Illness, injury[1], love, lost moments of true greatness and sheer[2] stupidity all occur to test the limits of your soul. Without these small tests, if they be events, illnesses or relationships, life would be like a smoothly paved, straight, flat road to nowhere.

If someone hurts you, betrays you , or breaks you heart, forgive them. For they have helped you learn about trust and the importance of being cautious[3] to who you open your heart to.

If someone loves you, love them back unconditionally, not only because they love you, but because they are teaching you to love and opening your heart and eyes to things you would have never seen or felt without them.

Make every day count. Appreciate[4] every moment and take from it everything that you possibly can, for you may never be able to experience[5] it again.

Talk to people who you have never talked to before, and actually listen. Hold your head up because you have every right to. Tell yourself you are a great individual[6] and believe in yourself, for if you don't believe in yourself, no one else will believe in you either.

You can make of your life anything you wish. Create your own life and then go out and live.

任何事情的发生都是有原因的，没有什么事是纯粹出于巧合或机会的好坏而发生。疾病，伤痛，爱情，曾经的荣耀和愚蠢的事，所有这一切的发生都是对你灵魂的考验。如果没有各种各样事情的发生，疾病或关系的考验，生活将会像一条已被铺就却没有目的地的平坦小路。

如果有人伤害了你，欺骗了你，让你心碎，原谅他们吧！至少他们让你学会了如何信任他人，他们让你懂得当你敞开心扉与人交流时，谨慎是多么重要。

如果有人爱你，你也无条件地去爱他们吧！因为他们不仅爱你，并让你也学会了爱，让你敞开心扉去感受你从未感受过的，睁开双眼去看你未曾看到过的。

珍惜每一天吧。把握生命中的每一刻，尽可能收获最多，因为时间将一去不复返。

与你从未交谈过的人聊聊吧，确切地说，是倾听。昂起你的头，因为你有权利这么做。告诉自己你是一个多么了不起的人，相信自己，因为如果连你自己都不相信自己，别人也就不会相信你了。

你可以按照你所期望的那样创造你自己的生活，活出自我。

❶ injury
/ˈɪndʒərɪ/
n. 伤害，损害
❷ sheer /ʃɪə/
adj. 绝对的，完全的
❸ cautious
/ˈkɔːʃəs/
adj. 谨慎的，极小心的
❹ appreciate
/əˈpriːʃɪeɪt/
v. 欣赏
❺ experience
/ɪkˈspɪərɪəns/
v. 体验
❻ individual
/ˌɪndɪˈvɪdʒʊəl/
n. 个人

Why does my foot fall asleep?

为什么我的脚要睡觉？

> *If you want to keep your feet awake and kick-ing, don't sit on them or put them in other posi-tions where you're squashing the nerves.*

> 如果你想让你的脚保持清醒，那就别坐在脚上或是做出会压迫神经的姿势。

Jenna had been coloring for almost 25 minutes when she leaned over her paper to put on the finishing touches. She had one leg tucked[1] under her, and when the bell rang and she tried to stand up, she felt something funny. Or was it that she didn't feel something — because her foot was asleep!

If you've ever sat on your foot for a while like Jenna or crossed your leg for a long time, you've probably felt the sensation[2] of the sleepy foot. It seems like there's no feeling in your foot, and it may feel heavy and lifeless or like "pins[3] and needles." But why would your foot fall asleep?

It has nothing to do with your foot wanting to catch up on some rest. And it's not that you've kept the blood from going to your foot and cut off your circulation, either. Instead, it's your nerves that are to blame. Nerves are like tiny threads that run through your whole body, and they receive messages from the brain and send messages back. When you sit on your foot, you temporarily compress[4], or squash, the nerves in that area. The brain isn't able to communicate to nerves that are squashed, and so for the moment, the connection is cut off and you don't feel anything. It's kind of like a phone call where your friend hangs up and you haven't yet: your brain is saying "hello," but your foot can't hear it.

After you stand up or uncross your legs and the nerves are no longer compressed, the feeling in your foot soon comes back. It might feel a bit tingly as this happens, like pins and needles or

为了这幅画的收笔，简已经着色 25 分钟了。她盘着腿，当铃声响起她想站起来时，她觉得很有趣。或者说她觉得很奇怪——她的脚睡觉了。

如果你像简那样坐在脚上很长一段时间或盘腿盘了好长时间，你可能会觉得你的脚已昏昏欲睡了。似乎是你的脚没感觉，或感到沉重麻木，或像"针扎"那样。但为什么你的脚会睡觉呢？

这似乎和脚想要休息没什么关系。这也不是你的血一直流向脚而你又阻断了这种流通。相反，原因在于你的神经。神经像微小的细线遍布你的全身，它们从大脑接受信息并做出反应。当你坐在脚上的时候，你暂时地挤压着那里的神经。大脑就无法与被挤压的神经进行交流，所以联系暂时被切断了，你就没有感觉了。这就像你朋友已挂断了电话而你还没有：你的大脑还在说"你好"，而你的脚却没听到。

在你站起来后或展开盘着的腿时，神经不再受到挤压，脚的感觉很快就恢复了。刚开始会有种刺痛的感觉，就像针扎一样或比那更痛苦一点。但这只是几秒钟而已，因为神经恢复了正常，而且不会伤害到身体。

担心你睡觉的脚吗？完全没必要担

❶ **tuck** /tʌk/
v. 折起
❷ **sensation**
/sen'seɪʃn/
n. 感觉
❸ **pin** /pɪn/
n. 别针；大头针
❹ **compress**
/kəm'pres/
v. 压缩

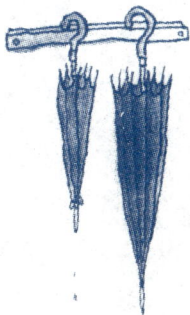

even a bit painful. But it only lasts a few seconds as the connection returns to normal, and it won't hurt your body.

Worried about your sleepy feet? You don't need to be — everyone's foot falls asleep once in a while and it's rare for it to mean there is something wrong in a kid's body. If you want to keep your feet awake and kicking, don't sit on them or put them in other positions where you're squashing[5] the nerves[6].

心——每个人的脚都会偶尔睡觉，这很少意味着你的身体出了什么问题。如果你想让你的脚保持清醒，那就别坐在脚上或是做出会压迫神经的姿势。

⑤ squash
/skwɒʃ/
v. 压烂；挤压
⑥ nerve /nɜːv/
n. 神经

Wait for the brick
等待砖块

Don't go through life so fast that someone has to throw a brick at you to get your attention!

生活中不要过于急躁，以至于别人不得不向你扔砖块来吸引你的注意力！

A young and successful executive[1] was traveling down a neighborhood street, going a bit too fast in his new Jaguar. He was watching for kids darting out from between parked cars and slowed down when he thought he saw something. As his car passed, no children appeared; Instead, a brick smashed[2] into the Jag's side door! He slammed on the brakes and drove the Jag back to the spot where the brick had been thrown. The angry driver then jumped out of the car, grabbed the nearest kid and pushed him up against a parked car, shouting, "What was that all about and who are you?

Just what the heck are you doing?

That's a new car and that brick you threw is going to cost a lot of money.

Why did you do it? "

The young boy was apologetic[3]. "Please mister ... please, I'm sorry... I didn't know what else to do," he pleaded.

"I threw the brick because no one else would stop..."

With tears dripping down his face and off his chin, the youth pointed to a spot just around a parked car. "It's my brother," he said.

"He rolled off the curb and fell out of his wheelchair[4] and I

一个年轻有为的官员开着美洲虎顺着邻近街道的游览，车速有点快。他正看着孩子们从停着的车中间往外冲。当他觉得他看见什么东西时，便放慢车速。当他的车路过时，孩子们并没有出现。可是，一块砖头砸破了他那辆美洲虎的门。他猛地刹住车，然后把他的美洲虎开回到刚才有人扔砖头的地方。气愤的司机跳出汽车，抓住最近的一个小孩把他推到一辆停在旁边的车上。喊道："怎么回事？你是谁？

你到底在干些什么？

那是辆新车，你向它扔砖头要赔很多钱的。

你为什么这么干？"

男孩非常歉疚。"请先生…请，非常对不起…我不知道还有什么别的办法，"他恳求道。

"我扔砖块是因为没有人愿意停下来…"

泪水顺着他的脸流到下巴上，少年指着一辆停着的车旁说："他是我哥哥。"

"他从围栏上翻下来，摔出了轮椅，我扶不动他。"

这时的他哭泣着问这个被惊呆了的官员："你愿意帮我把他扶回轮椅吗？他受伤了，对我来说他太重了，扶不动。"

官员被他的话感动了，努力把冒出的火压回去，他立刻把那个残疾的男孩扶回轮椅。

❶ executive
/ɪɡˈzekjʊtɪv/
n. 行政官；执行者
❷ smash
/smæʃ/
v. 粉碎；击败
❸ apologetic
/əˌpɒləˈdʒetɪk/
adj. 道歉的；歉疚的
❹ wheelchair
/ˈwiːltʃeə/
n. 轮椅

can't lift him up."

Now sobbing, the boy asked the stunned executive, "Would you please help me get him back into his wheelchair? He's hurt and he's too heavy for me."

Moved beyond words, the driver tried to swallow the rapidly swelling[5] lump in his throat. He hurriedly lifted the handicapped boy back into the wheelchair, then took out his fancy handker-chief and dabbed at the fresh scrapes[6] and cuts. A quick look told him everything was going to be okay.

"Thank you and may God bless you," the grateful child told the stranger.

Too shook up for words, the man simply watched the little boy push his wheelchair-bound brother down the sidewalk toward their home. It was a long, slow walk back to the Jaguar. The damage was very noticeable, but the driver never bothered to repair the dented side door. He kept the dent there to remind him of this message: Don't go through life so fast that someone has to throw a brick at you to get your attention!

God whispers in our souls and speaks to our hearts. Some-times when we don't have time to listen. He has to throw a brick at us. It's our choice: Listen to the whisper ... or wait for the brick!

然后拿出他的花手绢轻轻地擦拭着男孩的伤口。他迅速的一瞥告诉男孩一切都会好起来的。

"谢谢你，愿上帝保佑你。"男孩对这个陌生人感激地说。

男孩的话让这个男人深受震憾，只是看着小男孩沿着人行道推着轮椅里的哥哥向家里走去。他很久才慢慢地回到他的美洲虎车上。车上的毁坏处很明显，但是这个司机却从来没有想着要去修那扇车门上面的凹痕。他要保留门上的那处凹痕来提醒他这样一个信息：生活中不要过于急躁，以至于别人不得不向你扔砖块来吸引你的注意力！

上帝向我们的灵魂低语，对我们的心灵讲话。有时候，我们没有时间去倾听，于是他不得不向我们扔上一块砖头。这就是我们的选择了：听他低语？还是等待那块砖头？

❺ **swelling**
/ˈswelɪŋ/
n. 增大；隆起；膨胀

❻ **scrape**
/skreɪp/
n. 擦伤

A box full of kisses
一盒子的吻

Daddy, it's not empty at all. I blew kisses into the box. They're all for you, Daddy.

爸爸,盒子不是空的。我向里面吹了很多个吻,都是送给你的,爸爸。

The story goes that some time ago, a man punished his 3-year-old daughter for wasting a roll of gold wrapping paper. Money was tight and he became infuriated[1] when the child tried to decorate[2] a box to put under the Christmas tree. Nevertheless, the little girl brought the gift to her father the next morning and said, "This is for you, Daddy."

The man was embarrassed[3] by his earlier overreaction, but his anger flared[4] again when he found out the box was empty. He yelled at her, stating, "Don't you know, when you give someone a present, there is supposed to be something inside?" The little girl looked up at him with tears in her eyes and cried, "Oh, Daddy, it's not empty at all. I blew kisses into the box. They're all for you, Daddy."

The father was crushed. He put his arms around his little girl, and he begged for her forgiveness.

Only a short time later, an accident took the life of the child. It is also told that her father kept that gold box by his bed for many years and, whenever he was discouraged, he would take out an imaginary kiss and remember the love of the child who had put it there.

In a very real sense, each one of us, as humans beings, have been given a gold container filled with unconditional[5] love and kisses... from our children, family members, friends, and God. There is simply no other possession, anyone could hold, more precious than this.

故事发生在很久以前。一位父亲惩罚三岁的女儿，因为女儿浪费了一卷金包装纸。当时他们家庭经济紧张，看到女儿将一卷金包装纸的盒子放在圣诞树下，父亲非常生气。圣诞节早上，小姑娘把那个小礼盒送给父亲："这是给你的，爸爸。"

父亲后悔不该那样处罚三岁的女儿，但当他发现礼盒是空的时，他又火冒三丈，大声嚷道："难道你不知道，送别人礼盒时，礼盒里应该放东西吗？"小姑娘泪水晶莹地看着父亲，委屈地哭道：爸爸，盒子不是空的，我向里面吹了很多个吻，都是送给你的，爸爸。

父亲简直要羞愧难当了，他张开双臂抱着小姑娘，乞求女儿的原谅。

不久以后，一场事故夺走了小姑娘的生命。据说后来父亲一直把那个礼盒放在自己床边，每当他感到沮丧时，他就拿出礼盒，想女儿送给他的爱和吻。

事实上，我们每个人都拥有一个金制容器，里面装满了无私的爱和吻，有儿女的，有家人的，有朋友的，也有上帝的。每一个人都拥有它，并不一定每个人都懂得如何珍惜它。

---

❶ **infuriate**
/ɪnˈfjʊərɪeɪt/
v. 激怒，使极为不满

❷ **decorate**
/ˈdekəreɪt/
v. 装饰

❸ **embarrassed**
/ɪmˈbærəst/
adj. 尴尬的

❹ **flare** /fleə/
v. 勃然大怒

❺ **unconditional**
/ˌʌnkənˈdɪʃənl/
adj. 无条件的

Life

生 活

Only you choose the way those hearts are affected, and those choices are what life's all about.

只要你可以选择触动他人内心的方法，
这些选择便构成了生活。

Life isn't about keeping score[1].

It's not about how many friends you have or how accepted you are.

Not about if you have plans this weekend or if you're alone.

It isn't about who you're dating, who you used to date[2], how many people you've dated, or if you haven't been with anyone at all.

It isn't about who you have kissed.

It's not about sex.

It isn't about who your family is or how much money they have.

Or what kind of car you drive.

Or where you are sent to school.

It's not about how beautiful or ugly you are.

Or what clothes you wear, what shoes you have on, or what kind of music you listen to.

It's not about if your hair is blonde, red, black, or brown or if your skin is too light or too dark.

Not about what grades you get, how smart you are, how smart everybody else thinks you are, or how smart standardized tests say you are.

It's not about representing your whole being on a piece of paper and seeing who will "accept the written you." LIFE JUST ISN'T?

But, life is about who you love and who you hurt.

It's about who you make happy or unhappy purposefully.

It's about keeping or betraying[3] trust.

It's about friendship, used as a sanctity[4] or a weapon.

It's about what you say and what you mean, maybe hurtful,

生活不是记分数。

它不是关于你有多少朋友或者你有多受欢迎。

不是关于这个周末你是否有计划还是独自一人。

不是关于你在和谁约会，曾和谁约会，和多少人约会过，或者根本就没和任何人约会过。

不是关于你曾吻过谁。

它也不是关于两性的。

它不是关于你的家庭中有谁，他们赚多少钱或你驾驶什么样的车或你在哪上学。

它不是关于你有多漂亮或多丑陋。

或者你穿什么样的衣服，什么样的鞋或听什么样的音乐。

它不是关于你的头发是金色的、红色的、黑色的、还是棕色的或你的皮肤是太白还是太黑。

它不是关于你得了多少分，你有多聪明，别人认为你有多聪明，或者智力标准测试认为你有多聪明。

它不是关于把代表你方方面面的情况列在一张纸上，然后看谁会"接受书面的你"。

生活不仅仅是这样。

但是，生活是你爱谁、你伤害了谁。

它是关于你故意逗谁开心或惹谁生气。

它是关于保持或摧毁信任。

它是关于友谊，将它作为尊严或武器。

它是关于你说什么和有何意图，或许它会带

① **score** /skɔː/
n. 得分，比分，计分

② **date** /deɪt/
n. 约会

③ **betray**
/bɪˈtreɪ/
v. 背叛

④ **sanctity**
/ˈsæŋktətɪ/
n. 神圣，崇高，圣洁

maybe heartening.

It's about starting rumors and contributing to petty gossip.

It's about what judgments you pass and why. And who your judgment are spread to.

It's about who you've ignored with full control and intention.

It's about jealousy, fear, ignorance, and revenge[5].

It's about carrying inner hate and love, letting it grow, and spreading it.

But most of all, it's about using your life to touch or poison other people's hearts in such a way that could have never occurred alone.

Only you choose the way those hearts are affected[6], and those choices are what life's all about.

来伤痛或许振奋人心。

它是关于散布谣言、流长蜚短。

它是关于你的判断是什么和为什么，以及你
是对谁做的判断。

它是关于你故意忽视谁。

它是关于妒忌、恐惧、忽略和报复。

它是关于释放、增加内心的爱与恨。

但最重要的是，它是关于用你的生活去感动
或去毒害其他人的心，好让你的心不再独自
悲欢。

只有你可以选择触动他人内心的方法，这些
选择便构成了生活。

❺ revenge

/rɪˈvendʒ/

v. 报复，报仇

❻ affected

/əˈfektɪd/

adj. 感动的，动心
的

Trying to avoid selling out in the US

在形形色色的
文化中保持自我

They are searching for meaning in life, something beyond the routine, traditional lifestyle.

他们想寻求生活的真正意义，寻求超越常规、超越传统的一种新的生活方式。

Many young people with alternative[1] lifestyles hang out in coffee shops, but they could spend their whole life without going to a Starbucks.

Many are anti-establishment and against conformity[2]. They prefer small, privately owned places with locally done art on the walls, and good music over the speakers, or sometimes a local band playing.

Counterculture[3] is, as its name suggests, the opposite of pop culture ('counter-', from Latin: contrary; think of counter-revolutionary). Members of this group are not impressed with the flashy, promoted music videos and the pointless mega-movies. More popular are musicians with something important to say, often about politics or social problems, especially among the more radical. They realize that there is more to life than money, and are drawn to artists, musicians, and writers who have avoided "selling out" (giving in to marketed behavior, making their work less controversial[4] to sell to a wider audience for more money).

The radical appearance of the counterculture can sometimes shock the more conservative members of society. Dyed hair, facial piercing, controversial T-shirts, and crazy accessories.

They can get stared at by older people and use alternative political slogans[5]. For example like "Support our troops — bring them home". This is an ironic comment (the standard posters read "Support our troops", meaning support them overseas) in

许多年轻人的生活方式与众不同，他们经常光顾小饭馆，但可能一辈子都不进星巴克。

这些年轻人不愿因循守旧，循规蹈矩，他们更乐意生活在狭小的私人空间里。四周墙上贴满具有地方色彩的图片，他们更喜欢边听优美音乐边聊天，有个地方乐队伴奏也不错。

反文化，顾名思义，也就是主流文化的对立面（counter：来自于拉丁词 contrary，很容易让人联想到反革命 counterrevolutionary），反文化者，对炫耀庸俗的音乐电视，打打闹闹的大型宽幕电影丝毫不感兴趣，相反，经常唱一些激进的政治或社会问题的音乐家却很受他们欢迎。金钱并不是生活中最重要的东西，基于这样的认识，他们崇拜那些没有因金钱利益而出卖灵魂的艺术家、音乐家、作家。

有时他们夸张的衣着打扮很让社会的保守派吃惊。比如：染发、面部穿孔、奇形怪状的 T 恤衫，稀里古怪的小玩意儿。

老一代人对他们的行为感到惊愕，他们甚至还有独有的政治口号。例如："支持我们的军队——撤兵回老家。"这是个非常具有讽刺性的口号。（因为通常情况下海报刊登：支持我们的军队——继续进军海外）他们以

❶ alternative
/ɔːlˈtɜːnətɪv/
n./adj. 二选一；两者选其一的
❷ conformity
/kənˈfɔːmɪtɪ/
n. 一致，遵从
❸ counterculture
/ˌkaʊntəˈkʌltʃə/
n. 反文化
❹ controversial
/ˌkɒntrəˈvɜːʃl/
adj. 有争议的
❺ slogan
/ˈsləʊgən/
n. 口号

protest against the US invasion of Iraq. Another example, "Tax the rich", a comment on the growing gap between the rich and the poor.

Still, beliefs and values may differ, depending on the person, or where he or she lives. Some want to shock the community to make people see that there is more to a person than their appearance, that life is not "skin-deep". Others are involved in politics and call for accountability (responsibility) in government, or supporting a different party, for example the Greens.

They are searching for meaning in life, something beyond the routine, traditional lifestyle. Many still go to college, to learn about the world, so that they might improve it. Others just drop out to do whatever interests them, for example, to be a carpenter.

Many mainstream[6] people think that members of the counter-culture are lazy drug users or just like to shock people and that, sooner or later, they will "grow out of it". However, some symbols that go against society have become integrated into the mainstream. Rap artists, for example, have managed to reach large audiences, even though the original appeal was to disaffect young people.

此来反对美国对伊战争。又如："向富人征税"，表达了他们对美国贫富差距加大的担忧。

当然，因每个人的性格或生存环境不同，他们的信仰和价值观也不尽相同，有的人想一鸣惊人以此来证明外表并不决定人的一切。生活不是人们想象的那样肤浅。有的人参与政治活动、呼吁政府对民众的责任，或支持另外一个党派，如环保激进党派。

他们想寻求生活的真正意义，寻求超越常规超越传统的一种新的生活方式。很多人仍然选择上大学，从书中了解世界，梦想改变世界，也有一部分人退学去做自己喜欢做的事情（如当个木匠）。

主流文化者认为反文化者都是懒惰的吸毒者，他们行为乖张，只是为吸引注意力，并断言他们迟早会被社会淘汰。然而一些迹象表明，他们不仅没有被主流文化淘汰，反而成为主流文化的一部分，比如，一些说唱艺术家最初只是为了迎合满腹牢骚的年轻人，结果却赢得了大量的听众。

❻ mainstream
/ˈmeɪnstriːm/
n. 主流

Cheating

作　弊

Copying someone else's words or work and saying they're yours is a type of cheating called plagiarizing.

抄袭他人的话语或作品并声称是自己的成果是剽窃行为。

Just as the teacher hands out the spelling test, you see Megan pull out a small piece of paper with a lot of little scribbling[1] on it. Megan tucks the note into her closed fist, but soon takes it out again. While she's taking the test, you see her looking back and forth between the teacher and her paper. There's no mistaking it — she's cheating.

What Exactly Is Cheating?

Cheating is when a person misleads, deceives[2], or acts dishonestly on purpose. For kids, cheating may happen at school, at home, or while playing a sport. If a baseball team is for kids who are 8 or younger, it's cheating for a 9-year-old to play on the team.

At school, in addition to cheating on a test, a kid might cheat by stealing someone else's idea for a science project or by copying a book report off the Internet and turning it in as if it's his or her original work. Copying someone else's words or work and saying they're yours is a type of cheating called plagiarizing[3].

How do people cheat?

Cheating can happen in a lot of different ways. Megan is doing it by sneaking answers to a test, but it's also cheating to break the rules of a game or contest or to pretend[4] something is yours when it isn't. When people cheat, it's not fair to other people, like the kids who studied for the test or who were the true winners of a game or contest.

It's tempting to cheat because it makes difficult things seem

当老师进行拼写测试时，你会看到麦格拿出一张写得密密麻麻的纸条，把纸条攥在手心里，然后把纸条打开，考试时你发现她左顾右盼，一会看看老师一会看看试卷毫无疑问：她在作弊。

究竟何为作弊？作弊是一个人故意误导、欺骗他人或者是行为不诚实，孩子们的作弊行为可能发生在家里，学校，或者做游戏的过程当中。如果一个儿童网球队要求其队员年龄在8岁或8岁以下，那么9岁儿童参加这个球队就是作弊行为了。

在学校除考试作弊外，学生还可能在科学实验上抄袭他人作法或从网上下载读书报告，然后变成自己的东西，好像那些原本就是他们智慧的结晶。抄袭他人的话语或作品并声称是自己的成果是剽窃行为。

如何作弊

作弊的方式有多种多样。麦格抄袭试题答案是作弊行为。但是如果违反了游戏或者比赛规则，或者假称不属于你的东西为你所有也算是作弊行为。当人们作弊时，必然对其他人不公平。比如那些为了考试真正学习了的孩子，那些游戏或者比赛中本应该是真正的获胜者。

人们作弊的心理动机是想走捷径（如不

❶ scribbling
/'skrıblıŋ/
n. 乱涂，乱画
❷ deceive
/dı'siːv/
v. 欺骗
❸ plagiarize
/'pleıdʒəraız/
v. 抄袭，剽窃
❹ pretend
/prı'tend/
v. 假装

easy, like getting all the right answers on the test. But it doesn't solve the problem of not knowing the material and it won't help on the next test — unless the person cheats again.

Sometimes it may seem like cheaters have it all figured out. They can watch TV instead of studying for the spelling test. But other people lose respect for cheaters and think less of them. The cheaters themselves may feel bad because they know they are not really earning that good grade. And, if they get caught cheating, they will be in trouble at school, and maybe at home, too.

Why kids cheat

Some kids cheat because they're busy or lazy and they want to get good grades without spending the time studying. Other kids might feel like they can't pass the test without cheating. Even when there seems to be a "good reason" for cheating, cheating isn't a good idea.

If you were sick or upset about something the night before and couldn't study, it would be better to talk with the teacher about this. And if you don't have enough time to study for a test because of swim practice, you need to talk with your parents about how to balance[5] swimming and school.

A kid who thinks cheating is the only way to pass a test needs to talk with the teacher and his or her parents so they can find some solutions[6] together. Talking about these problems and working them out will feel better than cheating.

用思考可以打满分）。但这并不能从根本上解决问题，也不会对下次考试有任何帮助——除非下一次继续作弊。

有时候作弊者好像也能想明白。他们可以去看电视，而不必为了拼写考试去学习。当然同时他们也失去了周围人的尊重和良好评价。作弊者尽管得了高分，但是他们自我感觉也并不良好，因为他们知道那并不是他们的真实成绩。一旦作弊被发现，他们在学校，也有可能在家里都陷于困境。

孩子们为什么作弊

有些孩子作弊是因为他们太忙或太懒。而且他们不想好好学习还想取得好成绩。其他孩子是因为觉得不作弊就通不过考试。就算他们有多么"好"的理由，作弊也算不上是个好办法。如果你考前晚上因某件事心烦不安，学不进去，最好与老师就此事谈谈。如果你是因为游泳训练而没有足够时间准备考试，你需要跟你的家长商量一下如何协调一下游泳和学习的时间。

如果一个孩子认为作弊是通过考试的惟一途径的话，一定要和他（她）的老师家长谈谈，共同寻找解决问题的办法。开诚布公地和他们谈谈这些问题并找到解决的方法比作弊让人感觉好得多。

❺ balance
/ˈbæləns/
v. 平衡
❻ solution
/səˈluːʃn/
n. 解决问题的方法

Avoiding bad dreams

梦你所想

A new gadget has been designed to help people shape their nightly sleep.

有一种新的仪器可以帮助人们做梦，也就是说做梦者可以梦其所想

A NEW gadget[1] has been designed to help people shape their nightly sleep. That means dreams could be full of whatever the sleeper desires — whether it be a date with a movie star or winning gold at the Olympics.

It stands just under one meter tall and has been dubbed[2] Yumemi Kobo — Japanese for "dream workshop" — by its creator, Japanese toy maker Takara.

The dream machine comes with a voice recorder, an array of lights, a picture frame, a fragrance dispenser, a selection of internally stored background music, two speakers and a timer.

These components work in conjunction[3] to allow the user to design dreams through multi-sensory stimuli: scents, sounds and more.

"The general concept is you'd sit down with it for a few minutes before you go to bed," said Peter Harwood, senior marketing manager with Takara USA. Once this is done, he says, you are ready to visit Venice in your dreams.

First, you attach a photograph or image of a desired dream to the Yumemi Kobo. Then you concentrate on the image, playing out the desired dream in your head while making a voice recording of key words describing the fantasy.

Next you insert one of the dream machine's scents in the fragrance dispenser and select accompanying music from the

有一种新的仪器可以帮助人们做梦，也就是说做梦者可以梦其所想：比如和明星约会或者在奥运会上赢上一枚金牌什么的。这个仪器大约有一米高，被称为：Yumemi Kobo，日语的意思是造梦工厂。它的发明者是日本的玩具商Takara。

这个造梦机器由一个录音机，一排彩灯，一个画框，一个香水喷洒器，一系列挑选出来的背景音乐，两个话筒和一个计时器组成。

这些部件共同起作用可以让使用者通过各种感官刺激如嗅觉，听觉等设计自己的各种梦境。

"整个程序是你在睡前和它坐上一会儿"皮特·哈伍德说。他是Takara驻美国的销售部总经理。"然后你就可以在你的梦中游览威尼斯了。"他如是说。

首先，你在造梦机器上贴上你梦想中的图片或者形象。然后把注意力集中在它上面，在脑中想象你所希望的梦境，同时把描述你幻想的关键词录制下来。

接下来你把造梦机器中的一种香味插入香水散发器中，再从仪器中的数据库中选择一种伴奏音乐。

"这些选择的依据是科学家对梦的研究结

❶ gadget
/ˈɡædʒɪt/
n. (尤指电子，机械装置的)小发明，小玩意儿
❷ dub /dʌb/
v. 给……某种称号
❸ conjunction
/kənˈdʒʌŋkʃn/
n. 连接，联合

tracks in the device's database.

"These selections are based on sleep research by scientists who have an idea of what fragrances and music relaxes people the most," Harwood says.

Now, you're ready to <u>hit the sack</u>[4]. You turn on the dream machine and it starts to ease you into sleep with soft lights and gentle songs.

For the next eight hours, while you snooze[5], the device is set to activate periodically in accordance with your REM (rapid eye movement) sleep. That's the period associated with dreaming, when a sleeper's eyeballs jerk[6] rapidly.

"REM occurs for about an hour and a half. The machine estimates when most people achieve this," Harwood says.

This is when the dream controller is at its most active. It plays the music, releases the fragrance and repeats the recorded phrase to trigger the desired dream.

Eight hours later, the dream machine gently awakens you with dim lights and soft music.

Craig Webb, executive director of The Dreams Foundation, a group that promotes sleep research, said it is possible to guide the content of dreams. But he sees a drawback to the Yumemi Kobo.

果。他们认为最让人感到放松的是香水和音乐。"哈伍德说。

现在就可以准备就寝了。你打开造梦机器，然后它开始用轻音乐和温柔的歌声把你轻松地带入梦乡。

接下来的8个小时中，当你打呼噜时，仪器可以根据眼球跳动的次数阶段性地激活你的睡眠。当睡眠者的眼球迅速跳动时，说明他正处于做梦状态。

"眼球迅速跳动的时间大约持续一个半小时。机器可以估计出大部分人在何时处于这种阶段。"哈伍德说。

这是做梦控制器最活跃的时候，它播放音乐，散发香味，重复录制的词语来促使你进入期待的梦境。

8小时后，造梦机器会用淡淡的灯光和轻柔的音乐把你唤醒。

Craig Webb，这个以促进睡眠研究为目的的梦境机构的总经理说，这种机器有可能引导你的做梦内容，但他同时也看到了Yumemi Kobo的不足之处。

"其中最大的缺陷就是它无法辨别眼球迅速跳动的时间，"Webb说："眼球快速跳动会随着你的运动量与休息量的变化而大幅度变化。"

④ hit the sack
(美俚) 就寝，上床睡觉
⑤ snooze
/snuːz/
v. 小睡，假寐，打盹
⑥ jerk /dʒɜːk/
v. 急拉，猛扭

"One big limitation is that it can't tell when REM occurs," Webb said. "REM varies widely depending on how much exercise or how much rest you've had."

Webb also voiced concern that the machine requires a person to trust something that is affecting natural body cycles.

So far, Takara has tested its dream machine only on employees. The inventors admit they have some adjusting to do before the device hits the market. But Harwood said the preliminary results have been promising, indicating that the gadget can greatly improve the odds of experiencing a desired dream.

　　Webb也表示，他担心这种机器会使人相信那些影响人体自然循环的东西。

　　到目前为止，Takara只是在它的员工身上做过测验。它的发明者承认在这种仪器投入市场以前还要做一些调整。不过哈伍德说初步结果表明它很有前景。他指出，这个小仪器可以大大提高体验自己所希望的梦境的可能性。

Love and time

爱与时间

Only Time is capable of understanding how valuable Love is.

因为只有时间才能理解爱是多么重要。

Once upon a time, there was an island where all the feelings lived: Happiness, Sadness, Knowledge, and all of the others, including Love. One day it was announced[1] to the feelings that the island would sink[2], so all constructed[3] boats and left. Except for Love.

Love was the only one who stayed. Love wanted to hold out until the last possible moment.

When the island had almost sunk, Love decided to ask for help.

Richness was passing by Love in a grand[4] boat. Love said,

"Richness, can you take me with you? "

Richness answered, "No, I can't. There is a lot of gold and silver in my boat. There is no place here for you."

Love decided to ask Vanity[5] who was also passing by in a beautiful vessel. "Vanity, please help me! "

"I can't help you, Love. You are all wet and might damage my boat," Vanity answered.

Sadness was close by, so Love asked, "Sadness, let me go with you."

"Oh . . . Love, I am so sad that I need to be by myself! "

从前有一个小岛，岛上居住着各种各样的情感：快乐、伤心、智慧和其它情感，也包括爱。有一天，情感们听说小岛要沉海了，几乎所有的情感都乘船离开了小岛。只有爱没有离开小岛，它要坚持到最后一刻。

小岛就要沉海了，爱决定求救。

财富大哥乘一只华丽的船从爱的身旁经过，爱求救道："财富大哥，救救我，带我走吧。"

财富大哥答道："不好意思，船上放着很多金银财宝，没有你坐的地方。"

这时虚荣大姐乘一只漂亮的船从爱的身旁经过，爱决定向虚荣大姐求救："虚荣大姐，请帮个忙吧。"

"我帮不了你，爱小妹，你浑身湿漉漉的，会把我的船压坏的，"虚荣大姐答道。

当伤心大哥经过爱身旁时，爱又求救："伤心大哥，让我跟你走吧"。

"噢，爱小妹，我心情不好，想一个人静静"。

快乐大姐从爱身旁经过，可是她太高兴了，压根就没听见爱小妹的求救声。

突然，从远处传来一个声音："嗨，爱小妹，我带你走"。爱小妹太激动太高兴了，她甚至没有问老者会带她去哪里就上船了。到

① announce
/əˈnaʊns/
v. 宣布，宣告
② sink /sɪŋk/
vi. 下沉，倒下
③ construct
/kənˈstrʌkt/
v. 建筑，建设，构筑
④ grand /grænd/
adj. 华丽的，庄严的
⑤ vanity
/ˈvænətɪ/
n. 虚荣

Happiness passed by Love, too, but she was so happy that she did not even hear when Love called her.

Suddenly, there was a voice, "Come, Love, I will take you." It was an elder. So blessed and overjoyed, Love even forgot to ask the elder where they were going. When they arrived at dry land, the elder went her own way. Realizing how much was owed the elder,

Love asked Knowledge, another elder, "Who Helped me? "

"It was Time," Knowledge answered.

"Time? " asked Love. "But why did Time help me? "

Knowledge smiled with deep wisdom and answered, "Because only Time is capable of understanding how valuable[6] Love is."

岸后，老者什么也没说就走了。爱小妹非常
感激这位老者。

　　爱小妹问智慧爷爷："是谁帮助了我?"

　　"是时间，"智慧爷爷答道。

　　"时间?"爱小妹疑惑不解。"时间为什么
要帮我呢?"

　　智慧爷爷答道："因为只有时间才能理解
爱是多么重要"。

❻ valuable

/ˈvæljʊəbl/

adj. 有价值的

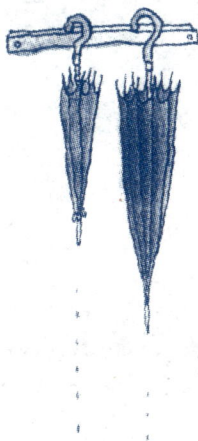

Why does hair turn gray?

为什么头发会变花白？

From the time a person notices a few gray hairs, it may take more than 10 years for all of that person's hair to turn gray.

从一个人第一次发现自己有白头发开始，大约10多年后他的头发才会全部变花白。

Have you ever watched your mom try to cover the gray in her hair with a tiny[1] bottle of hair coloring? Have you wondered why your granddad has a full head of silver hair when in old pictures it used to be dark brown? Getting gray, silver, or white hair is a natural part of growing older, and here's why.

Each hair on our heads is made up of a shaft[2] — the colored part we see growing out of our heads — and a root at the bottom that keeps the hair anchored under the scalp. The root of every strand of hair is surrounded by a tube of tissue under the skin that is called the hair follicle. Each hair follicle contains a certain number of pigment cells.

These pigment cells continuously produce a chemical called melanin[3] that gives the growing shaft of hair its color of brown, blonde, red, and anything in between. Melanin is the same stuff that makes our skin's color fair or darker and helps determines whether a person will burn or tan in the sun. The dark or light color of someone's hair depends on how much melanin each hair contains.

As we get older, the pigment cells in our hair follicles[4] gradually die. When there are fewer pigment cells in a hair follicle, that strand of hair will no longer contain as much melanin and will become a more transparent color — like gray, silver, or white — as it grows. As people continue to get older, fewer and fewer of these pigment cells will be around to produce melanin, and the hair will eventually look completely gray.

你是否见过你妈妈拿着一小瓶染发剂在染她那花白的头发？你会好奇为什么你的爷爷有一头银发而在老相片里他的头发却是深棕色的？头发变花白，变成银色最后满头白发是人走向老年的自然过程的一部分，下面说的就是原因。

每根头发都是由杆状物——在头上我们可以看见的有颜色的那部分——和使头发植于头皮下的根部构成的。每根头发的根部都被皮肤下一个叫小囊的组织包围着。每个发囊都包含着一定数量的色素细胞。

这些色素细胞不断地产生一种叫黑色素的化学元素。这些化学元素给了头发颜色——棕色，金色，红色和任何两种间的颜色。黑色素也是一种使我们的皮肤变黑或变白，决定我们的皮肤在太阳下能否被晒黑的物质。每根头发包含黑色素的多少决定了一个人头发颜色的深浅。

当我们一天天变老的时候，发囊里的色素细胞就逐渐死了。当发囊里的色素细胞变得为数不多的时候，头发里的黑色素就少了，而变成了更透明的颜色——灰色，银色和白色。随着人们继续变老，能提供黑色素的色素细胞越来越少了，头发也会最终变得全白了。

人们在任何年龄段都可能有灰白的头发。

❶ tiny /ˈtaɪnɪ/
adj. 微小的；很小的

❷ shaft /ʃɑːft/
n. 轴；杆状物；箭杆

❸ melanin /ˈmelənɪn/
n. (生化)黑色素；黑蛋白

❹ follicle /ˈfɒlɪkl/
n. (医)小囊；滤泡

People can get gray hair at any age. Some people go gray at a young age — as early as when they are in high school or college — whereas others may be in their 30s or 40s before they see that first gray hair. How early we get gray hair is determined by our genes. This means that most of us will start having gray hairs around the same age that our parents or grandparents first did.

Other things have been linked to getting gray hair earlier in life. Poor nutrition (especially not getting enough B vitamins), thyroid problems, anemia, and even smoking can all contribute to the body's aging process that causes gray hair. Some diseases, such as AIDS or treatments for cancer[5], can also make people's hair turn gray while they are young.

Gray hair is more noticeable in people with darker hair because it stands out, but people with naturally lighter hair are just as likely to "go gray." From the time a person notices a few gray hairs, it may take more than 10 years for all of that person's hair to turn gray.

Some people think that a big shock or trauma[6] can turn a person's hair white or gray overnight, but scientists don't really believe that this happens. But just in case, try not to freak out your parents too much. You don't want to be blamed for any of their gray hairs!

有些人在很年轻的时候——高中或大学时就有灰白头发了，而有些人可能到了三四十岁才发现自己的第一根白发。我们在什么时候会有白头发是由我们的基因决定的。那就是说我们大多数人都会在我们父母或祖父母有白头发的那个年龄阶段出现白头发。

也有其他一些因素会导致我们在很早出现白发。营养不良（尤其是缺乏维生素B），甲状腺问题，贫血，甚至吸烟也会促成我们身体的衰老过程而导致白发出现。还有一些疾病如爱滋病或治疗癌症的过程也会使许多人在年轻时就有白发了。

深色头发的人有白头发会更引人注意，因为比较醒目，但有人的头发本来就是浅色也同样也有可能会"变白"。从一个人第一次发现自己有白头发开始，大约10多年后他的头发才会全部变白。

有些人认为巨大的打击或创伤会使一个人的头发一夜之间全部变白或变灰，但科学家却认为这不太可能。但是也要以防万一，尽量不要让父母因你过于受惊，你并不想让父母的黑发因你变白而受到指责吧！

❺ cancer
/ˈkænsə/
n. 癌症
❻ trauma
/ˈtrɔːmə/
n. （医）外伤；精神创伤

If I knew

假如我知道

Hold your loved ones close today, and whisper in their ear, that you love them very much and you'll always hold them dear.

今天就紧拥你心爱的人并在他们耳边轻语，你深深地爱着他们并将永远珍惜他们。

If I knew it would be the last time I'd see you fall asleep,

I would tuck[1] you in more tightly[2] and "pray the Lord, your soul to keep."

If I knew it would be the last time I'd see you walk out the door,

I would give you a hug and kiss you, and call you back for more.

If I knew it would be the last time I'd hear your voice lifted up in praise,

I would video tape each action and word, so I could play them back day after day.

If I knew it would be the last time I could spare an extra minute or so to stop and say "I love you," instead of assuming[3] you would know I do.

If I knew it would be the last time I would be there to share your day,

I'm sure you'll have so many more, so I can let just this one slip[4] away.

For surely there's always tomorrow to make up for an oversight[5], and we always get a second chance to make everything right.

There will always be another day, to say our "I love you", and certainly there's another chance to say our "Anything I can do?"

假如我知道这将是最后一次看着你睡去，

我将会更加紧紧地盖上你的被子"并祈求上帝，留住你的灵魂"。

假如我知道这将是最后一次看着你走出这扇门，

我将会拥抱亲吻你，更多地呼唤你回家。

假如我知道这将是最后一次听到你高声赞扬我的声音，

我将会用录像记下你的每一个动作与话语，这样我就可以每天重播它们。

假如我知道这将是我最后一次可以腾出多一分钟的时间留下来对你说声"我爱你"，就不会想当然的觉得你知道我会这样对你说的。

假如我知道这将是最后一次去你身边与你共度一天的时光，

我总确信你将会有更多的时光，我可以让这一天离我们而去。

因为肯定总会有明天来弥补过错，

我们总有第二次机会使一切美好。

总会有说"我爱你"的时间，当然也会有说"我可以帮你吗"的机会，

但是万一我想错了，而我只拥有今天，

我愿意说声我是多么的爱你并希望你铭记在心。

明天不会向任何人承诺什么，无论年老还是

❶ tuck
/tʌk/
v. 折，捐；（口语）安置于被窝里

❷ tightly
/ˈtaɪtlɪ/
adv. 紧紧地

❸ assume
/əˈsjuːm/
n. 假定，假设

❹ slip
/slɪp/
v. 滑到；错过

❺ oversight
/ˈəʊvəsaɪt/
n. 疏忽

But, just in case I might be wrong, and today is all I get,

I'd like to say how much I love you, and I hope we never forget.

Tomorrow is not promised to anyone, young or old alike, and today may be the last chance you get to hold your loved one tight.

So, if you're waiting for tomorrow, why not do it today?

For, if tomorrow never comes, you'll surely regret the day...

That you didn't take that extra time for a smile, a hug, or a kiss,
and you were too busy to grant someone, what turned out to be
their one last wish.

So, hold your loved ones close today, and whisper in their ear,
that you love them very much and you'll always hold them dear.

Take time to say "I'm sorry," "Please forgive[6] me," "thank you,"
or "its okay".

And if tomorrow never comes, you'll have no regrets about today.

年轻，

今天也许是你紧拥你心上人的最后一次机会。

那么如果你在等待明天，为什么不今天就行动？

因为假如明天永远不会来临，你一定会为今天后悔……

后悔你没有腾出哪怕多一分钟的时间去微笑，拥抱，亲吻。

后悔你因太忙而没有帮别人实现也许是最后的愿望。

所以今天就紧拥你心爱的人并在他们耳边轻语，你深深地爱着他们并将永远珍惜他们。

腾出些时间说声"对不起""请原谅""谢谢"或"没关系"。

即使明天永不再来，你也不会因今天而后悔。

❻ forgive

/fəˈɡɪv/

v. 原谅

The four wives

四个妻子

Our soul is actually the only thing that follows us wherever we go.

无论我们走到哪里，灵魂都会跟随我们的。

There was a rich merchant who had 4 wives. He loved the 4th wife the most and adorned[1] her with rich robes and treated her to delicacies. He took great care of her and gave her nothing but the best.

He also loved the 3rd wife very much. He's very proud of her and always wanted to show off her to his friends. However, the merchant is always in great fear that she might run away with some other men.

He too, loved his 2nd wife. She is a very considerate[2] person, always patient and in fact is the merchant's confidante[3]. Whenever the merchant faced some problems, he always turned to his 2nd wife and she would always help him out and tide him through difficult times.

Now, the merchant's 1st wife is a very loyal partner and has made great contributions in maintaining[4] his wealth and business as well as taking care of the household. However, the merchant did not love the first wife and although she loved him deeply, he hardly took notice of her.

One day, the merchant fell ill. Before long, he knew that he was going to die soon. He thought of his luxurious[5] life and told himself, "Now I have 4 wives with me. But when I die, I'll be alone. How lonely I'll be!"

Thus, he asked the 4th wife, "I loved you most, endowed you with the finest clothing and showered great care over you. Now that I'm dying, will you follow me and keep me company?" "No way!"

一个商人有四个妻子。他最爱的是第四个妻子，他给她穿最漂亮的衣服，吃美味佳肴。他细心地照顾她，给她一切最好的东西。

他也非常爱第三个妻子。他以她为荣，带着她向朋友们炫耀。但是，商人总是害怕她会跟别人跑了。

他也爱第二个妻子，她非常体贴，耐心，实际上她是商人的红粉知己。每当商人遇到困难时，她总是向第二个妻子求助。她总是扶助他，帮他走过困难时期。

现在，他的第一个妻子是非常忠实的伴侣。她为了照顾家庭，守护他的财富和生意做出了巨大的贡献。但是，商人并不爱第一个妻子，尽管她深深地爱着他，可是他几乎不看她一眼。

有一天，商人病倒了。不久他就清楚自己将会很快死去。他想着自己奢华的生活，对自己说："现在我有四个妻子，但是我死后就我一个人了，我将会是多么的孤独啊！"

于是，他问他的第四个妻子："我最爱的人是你，给你最华丽的衣服，细致入微地体贴你。现在我将要死去，你愿意跟我去陪伴我吗？""不可能！"第四个妻子回答道，一句话也没多说就走了。

她的回答像一把利刃插在商人的心上。

① **adorn**
/əˈdɔːn/
v. 装饰，美化

② **considerate**
/kənˈsɪdərət/
adj. 为他人着想的

③ **confidante**
/ˌkɒnfɪˈdænt/
adj. 红粉知己

④ **maintain**
/meɪnˈteɪn/
v. 维持，保持

⑤ **luxurious**
/lʌɡˈʒʊərɪəs/
adj. 奢华的，奢侈的

replied the 4th wife and she walked away without another word.

The answer cut like a sharp knife right into the merchant's heart. The sad merchant then asked the 3rd wife, "I have loved you so much for all my life. Now that I'm dying, will you follow me and keep me company? " "No! " replied the 3rd wife. "Life is so good over here! I'm going to remarry when you die! " The merchant's heart sank and turned cold.

He then asked the 2nd wife, "I always turned to you for help and you've always helped me out. Now I need your help again. When I die, will you follow me and keep me company? " "I'm sorry, I can't help you out this time! " replied the 2nd wife. "At the very most, I can only send you to your grave." The answer came like a bolt of thunder and the merchant was devastated. Then a voice called out: "I'll leave with you. I'll follow you no matter where you go." The merchant looked up and there was his first wife. She was so skinny, almost like she suffered from malnutrition. Greatly grieved, the merchant said, "I should have taken much better care of you while I could have ! "

Actually, we all have 4 wives in our lives

The 4th wife is our body. No matter how much time and effort we lavish in making it look good, it'll leave us when we die.

The 3rd wife is our possessions[6], status and wealth. When we die, they all go to others.

于是伤心的商人问他的第三个妻子："我一生都爱着你。现在我快要死了，你愿意跟我去陪伴我吗？""不！"第三个妻子回答说："这里的生活那么美好！你死了以后我要再婚！"商人的心沉了下去，变冷了。

他又去问第二个妻子："我总是向你求助，而且你总是帮助我。现在我又需要你的帮助了。我死时，你愿意跟我去陪伴我吗？""对不起，这次我帮不了你了！"第二个妻子回答说，"我最多只能为你送葬。"她的回答像晴天霹雳一样，商人非常惊愕。这时传来一个声音："我愿意和你一起走，无论你去哪里我都会跟随着你。"商人抬头一看，是他的第一个妻子，她瘦骨嶙峋，几乎像遭受营养不良一样。商人非常悲痛，他说："当我有能力的时候，我应该更好地照顾你！"

实际上，在生活中，我们都有四个妻子。

第四个妻子是我们的身体。无论我们花费多长的时间多大的精力使它美丽，我们死去时它将会离开我们。

第三个妻子是我们的家产，地位，财富。当我们死去时，它们将随他人而去。

第二个妻子是我们的家庭和朋友。在我们活着的时候，无论他们和我们有多么亲近，他们最远也只能陪我们到坟墓。

❻ possession
/pəˈzeʃn/
n. 财产

The 2nd wife is our family and friends. No matter how close they had been there for us when we're alive, the furthest they can stay by us is up to the grave.

The 1st wife is in fact our soul, often neglected in our pursuit of material, wealth and sensual pleasure.

Guess what? Our soul is actually the only thing that follows us wherever we go. Perhaps it's a good idea to cultivate and strengthen it now rather than to wait until we're on our deathbed to lament[7].

第一个妻子是我们的灵魂，在我们追求物质、财富和感官的愉悦的时候却忽视了它。

无论我们走到哪里，灵魂都会跟随我们的。也许现在就培养它并使它坚强是个好主意，而不要等到临死时才去悔恨。

❼ lament

/ləˈment/

v. 为…感到痛惜

I'm growing up — but am I normal[1]?

我是在长大 ——
可是我正常吗？

The truth is, no human being ever came from a cookie cutter, so we all look different.

事实是，人们不会一模一样，所以我们每个人看起来都与别人不同。

Since your last birthday, a lot of things have changed. For one, you're much smarter than you were last year. That's obvious. Also, you have some new privileges — maybe a later bedtime or a bigger allowance[2]. Whatever the changes, you've probably been expecting them.

But there might have been some other changes — ones that you weren't ready for. Perhaps you've sprouted[3] 3 inches above everyone else in class. Or maybe they all did the sprouting and you still feel like a spud. Maybe you haven't gained a pound and you feel like a feather on the seesaw[4], or maybe you can't fit into your favorite pair of jeans. And now you're looking in the mirror, thinking only one thing: am I normal?

Everybody's different

First of all, what's normal? It can't mean the same, that's for sure. If it did, the world would be full of abnormal people! The next time you go to the mall, take a look around. You'll see tall people, short people, and people with broad shoulders, little feet, big stomachs, long fingers, stubby legs, and skinny arms... you get the idea. The truth is, no human being ever came from a cookie cutter, so we all look different. So really, different is normal!

Although we don't all appear the same, your looks are not a matter of chance. They are largely determined by your parents. When your parents created you, they passed on their genes — a kind of special code — and those genes helped to decide your size and shape, your eye color and hair texture, even whether you have

自从你过了上一次生日，许多事都变了。首先你比去年聪明了。那是很明显的。其次，你有了一些特权——也许是可以晚睡一会或是零花钱多了一点。无论变化是什么，你可能会很期待这些变化。

但或许还有其他一些变化——你还没对这些变化作好准备。可能你比班里每个人都高出 3 英寸。或许每个人都长高了，你却还是保持原来的个头。或许是你的体重连一磅都没长，还像个跷跷板上的羽毛，或许你长胖了，穿不上你最喜欢的那条牛仔裤了。你看着镜中的自己，只想着一件事：我正常吗？

每个人都是不同的

首先，什么是正常的？它不可能是与人毫无差别的，那是肯定的。如果是真的，那世界上就到处是不正常的人了。下次当你走进大厅的时候，向四周望一望。你会发现周围的人有高的、矮的、宽肩膀的、小脚的、大肚子的、长手指的、短粗腿的、细胳膊的……你就明白了。事实是，人们不会一模一样，所以我们每个人看起来都与别人不同。所以，不同才是正常的。

尽管我们看上去各不相同，你的容貌也不是偶然的。它们主要是由你的父母决定的。当你的父母把你带到这个世界上时，他们就

---

❶ normal
/'nɔ:ml/
adj. 正常的

❷ allowance
/ə'lauəns/
n. 津贴，补助，零用钱

❸ sprout
/spraut/
v. 长出

❹ seesaw
/'si:sɔ:/
n. 跷跷板

freckles. So obviously, there can't be a right or wrong way to look; there's only your way.

Small or tall

Height is just one of the thousands of features your genes[5] decide. In fact, because you have two parents, your genes act like a referee, giving you a height that usually lands somewhere between the height of each parent. Dr. Sajjad Yacoob, a doctor who treats kids in California, explains it like this: "If both parents are short, it doesn't necessarily mean you'll be short, but more than likely, you'll be somewhere in between the height of your mom and dad. You don't usually get kids who are much taller or smaller than their parents."

But genes don't decide everything. Your environment has something to do with how much you grow. For example, eating an unhealthy diet can keep you from growing to your full potential. Getting plenty of sleep, enough exercise, and nutrients are important to your rate of growth.

No doubt you're wondering what the right rate of growth is. It depends. Although on average kids grow about 2 inches a year between age 3 and when they start puberty[6], "there is no exact right rate of growth," says Dr. Yacoob. "What is important is that you progress at a rate that is right for you." And that rate should only be figured out by a doctor, someone who knows how your growth has progressed over the years. Two centimeters here and 2 inches there are not nearly as important as the height you're at now,

把基因传给了你——一种特殊的编码，这些基因决定了你的身高和体形，你眼睛的颜色和发质，甚至你的身上是否有痣。所以很明显，长相并没有什么对错，那只是你的特色而已。

高还是矮

　　身高只是你的基因所决定的千百个特征中的一个。实际上，你的父母是不同的两个人，因此基因就像个裁判，使你的身高通常介于你的父母之间。撒亚库博士，在加利福尼亚治疗孩子的一位医生这样解释："如果你的父母很矮，并不意味着你也会很矮，很可能你的身高会介于你父母的身高之间。不会有孩子比父母高很多或矮很多。"

　　但基因并不决定一切。你生活的环境也会和你的成长有很大关系。例如，健康的饮食会使你的成长达到你的全部潜能。充足的睡眠和锻炼以及营养均衡对你的成长的限度是极其重要的。

　　毫无疑问，你会关心到底成长的限度是多少呢。这要看情况，尽管从3岁到开始进入青春期，一般的孩子每年长2英寸，但撒亚库博士说："没有确定的限度，重要的是你以一种适合你自己的速度成长。"这个速度只能由你的医生判断出来，因为他了解你的成

⑤ gene /dʒiːn/
n. （生物）遗传基因

⑥ puberty /ˈpjuːbətɪ/
n. 青春期

how you've been growing up to this point, and what other changes your body may be going through.

Don't be scared if you seem to have grown a lot in a very short time. Everyone has a growth spurt[7] during puberty. The average age for starting puberty is about 10 for girls and about 11 for boys, but there's a wide range of normal — between 7 and 13 for girls and 9 and 15 for boys. You'll usually begin to notice that you're growing faster about a year or so after your body starts to show the first changes of puberty — breast development in girls and growth of the testicles and penis in boys. Remember: everybody is different and on slightly different timetables.

长过程。这儿长 2 厘米那儿长 2 英寸不如你现在的身高那么重要，也不如你如何长到现在的程度及你还要经历哪些变化那么重要。

如果你在短时间内长了一大截那也不要害怕。每个人在青春期都有自己的成长高峰。女孩子进入青春期的平均年龄大约是 10 岁，男孩子大约是 11 岁，但正常的幅度是很大的——女孩 7—13 男孩 9—15 都是正常的。当你发现你的身体出现了第一次青春期的变化——女孩乳房发育，男孩睾丸和阴茎变大时，你通常已猛长了一年了。记住：每个人都是不同的，也有略微不同的成长时间表。

7 spurt

/spɜːt/

n. 突然的加速，劲头的迸发

Where is the treasure[1]?

宝藏在哪儿?

Walk into the country, sit down beside the river, under a very beautiful tree, and think about me.

到效外散步,坐在河边,在漂亮的树下乘凉,想想我。

Gentleman Jim was put in prison for his crime. Now he sent his wife a tape, and the police made sure that there was some information[2] hidden in this tape. After some policemen had carefully listened to the tape, they didn't find any information. Clever readers, can you find the information after you "listen to" the tape?

Hello, my dear wife. I want you to listen very carefully to this recording. Play it over and over again, and enjoy all the beautiful things I want to remind you about. Don't worry about me, just think about the beautiful things, and I'm sure you will be very happy, and you will find something very comforting in my words. Are you ready? I want to remind you of some really happy memories. Do you remember the day when we first met? You were very beautiful. There was a lot of sunshine that day, do you remember? There aren't many girls who are very beautiful, are there? But you were lovely. And our children are very beautiful. Two lovely girls and a handsome boy, although they're all in prison now. I remember when our son was small, he had lovely blue eyes, and very beautiful gold curly[3] hair. Do you remember the toys he used to play with? I remember his Teddy Bear, and also some very beautiful bricks[4], which he used to play with on the bedroom floor. Those were happy days. Do you remember, dear wife, the first dance we went to? You wore a blue dress and you looked very beautiful in the moonlight, and we danced until the morning, and then I took you home on my motorbike. Your mother was waiting for us and she looked very beautiful. The next day I asked you to marry me. I didn't think your mother was very pleased. She wanted us to buy the house next to her, do you remember? But we wanted

狱中服刑的吉姆先生送给妻子一盒录音带，警方怀疑录音带中有秘密，认真地听了一遍录音带后，他们并没有发现什么可疑之处。聪明的读者，你能从下面的录音带中发现宝物在哪儿吗？

你好！我的爱妻，仔细地反复地听下面的录音，希望你能享受生活中那些美丽的漂亮的东西，不必过多担心我，多去想想生活中美好的东西吧！我相信你一定会快乐的，一定会从我的录音中得到慰藉。我们在一起度过的时光留下多少甜蜜的回忆。记得我们第一次见面的情景吗？你是那样迷人，那天阳光明媚，还记得吗？没有多少女孩子可以与你比美，不是吗？你是那样可人，还有我们的三个孩子。两个乖巧的姑娘和帅气十足的儿子，我时常想起儿子小时候那双蓝色的大眼睛，漂亮的金色的卷发。你还记得他经常玩的玩具吗？小熊泰迪，漂亮的积木，他经常在卧室地板上玩积木的。那些日子是多么美好！

我的爱妻，还记得我们第一次跳舞的情景吗？你穿着蓝色的连衣裙，在月光下显得那么美丽，我们跳了个通宵，然后我骑摩托车把你送回家，你母亲在门口等我们，她看上去也很美丽。第二天我向你求婚，我觉得

❶ treasure /ˈtreʒə/ n. 财宝
❷ information /ˌɪnfəˈmeɪʃn/ n. 信息，消息
❸ curly /ˈkɜːlɪ/ adj. 卷的
❹ brick /brɪk/ n. 砖头

a bigger house, with a very beautiful garden and we found one. I like our house very much. I remember coming home one day in the winter, and looking at our house. It looked very beautiful under the white snow, and I knew that you were waiting in the kitchen with a cup of hot soup, and my dear friend Ginger. Poor Ginger, he has been in prison too. He says that you are very beautiful. The important thing in prison is to have happy memories. And I've got wonderful memories. Do you remember Ginger's cat? It was a very beautiful big black cat. Ginger liked it very much. He bought it fish to eat, and a very beautiful red ribbon[5], which he tied around its neck. I always liked Ginger's cat. I'm sorry I did not want to see you when you came. I wanted to send you this message instead. When I come home, I will buy you some expensive perfume[6] or a very beautiful rose. Play this recording many times, and think carefully about my words. Think about what came after all these beautiful things, and walk into the country, sit down beside the river, under a very beautiful tree, and think about me.

Your loving Gentleman,
Jim.

当时你母亲很不悦。她想让我们买你家隔壁的那套房子，而咱俩想买更宽敞一点并带有一个漂亮花园的，后来我们买到了满意的房子，我非常喜欢咱们那套房子。有一年冬天我回家时，远远看见咱们的房子，在雪的映衬下更漂亮了。我还知道你手里端一碗热汤在厨房里等我。

记得我的好朋友吉格吗？可怜的吉格也在狱中服刑，他告诉我你比以前更好看了。在狱中最值得骄傲的是我有许多美好的回忆。对了，还有吉格的猫，那只漂亮的大黑猫。吉格非常喜欢它，给它买鱼，买脖子上系的红丝带，我也喜欢那只猫。非常抱歉你来探监时我不想见你而是给了你这盒录音带，出狱后，我会给你买上等的香水，漂亮的玫瑰花。反复听录音，记住我所说的话，除了这些美妙的回忆，还有更美好的事情等着你，到效外散步，坐在河边，在漂亮的树下乘凉，想想我。你的爱人：吉姆

⑤ ribbon
/ˈrɪbən/
n. 缎带，丝带
⑥ perfume
/ˈpɜ:fju:m/
n. 香水

Answer：Gold bricks are in the garden under a big rose tree.

答案：金砖（财宝）在花园的大玫瑰树下

Exercise your head

锻炼大脑

Study has found that working out regularly improves your mood, boosts your sense of self-esteem and even enhances the function of your brain.

研究发现：有规律的锻炼能改善心境、提高自信心，甚至能增强大脑的功能。

It goes without saying that exercise is good for your body, but what many don't realize is that it's also good for your mind. No, we don't mean that weight training will suddenly turn you into an Einstein — but study has found that working out regularly improves your mood, boosts your sense of self-esteem and even enhances the function of your brain.

As with other aspects[1] of the health connection between mind and body, scientists are only beginning to understand why physical workouts also provide a mental and emotional boost[2]. But many possibilities are already known, and new research is continually going forward. For those in search of mental as well as physical motivation, here are 12 extra reasons to begin a workout program for the new millennium.

1. Working out can give you a sense of exhilaration[3] and accomplishment, and the increased self-esteem that results from doing something you know is good for you.

2. Exercise causes your body to produce endorphins, the chemicals that dull pain and help produce what's known as the exercise high.

3. Weight-bearing exercise particularly raises your testosterone levels, which can help improve your mood, especially if your levels are naturally on the low side.

4. According to Harvard psychiatrist John J.Raety, M.d.,

毫无疑问，锻炼对身体有益，但许多人没有认识到锻炼也有益于头脑。不，我们并不是说练举重会一下子把你变得像爱因斯坦那样聪明。但大量的研究发现：有规律的锻炼能改善心境、提高自信心，甚至能增强大脑的功能。

如同身体健康与头脑健康在其他方面的联系一样，虽然科学家们才刚刚开始明白为什么锻炼身体能增进智力，改善情绪，但是许多可能的事已为人所知，新的研究也在进行中。对于那些在头脑方面和身体方面寻找促进因素的人，以下是在新千年里开始锻炼计划的12条附加理由。

1. 锻炼能产生愉悦感和成就感，而且做某种熟悉的活动能提高自信，这样对你有好处。

2. 锻炼能促使身体分泌内啡肽，内啡肽能缓解痛感，有助于产生所谓的运动快感。

3. 举重训练尤其能够提高睾丸素水平，从而帮助改善心境，特别是如果你的睾丸素水平天生较低。

4. 哈佛大学精神病医生，医学博士约翰·瑞特是一本关于精神错乱的《影子综合症》的合著者，他认为单单一次锻炼就能提高大脑中多巴胺血清素和去甲肾上腺素等抗忧郁的化学物质含量。

5. 如果情绪低落，锻炼能使你振作起来。

① **aspect**
/ˈæspekt/
n. 方面

② **boost** /buːst/
v. 提高

③ **exhilaration**
/ɪɡˌzɪləˈreɪʃn/
n. 高兴，活跃，兴奋

coauthor of a book on psychological disorders called S*hadow Syndromes*, a single workout can raise your brain's levels of antidepressant chemicals, such as dopamine, serotonin and nore pinephrine.

5. If you are feeling down, exercise may help pick you up. Although researchers disagree on this issue, one review of past studies found that long-term exercise, especially when it includes long-lasting, strenuous[4] training sessions, has about as much of an effect on depression as psychotherapy.(Of course, this doesn't mean you shouldn't seek therapy. If you believe you may be suffering from depression, the first thing to do is to consult a mental-health professional.)

6. Working out helps you deal with stress in your job, relationships or any area of life — possibly because exercise is a form of stress itself and helps condition your body to deal with it. When Australian researchers compared people who did 30 minutes of aerobic[5] exercise three times a week to those who practiced progressive-relaxation techniques, they found that the former group responded better to acute stress and had lower blood pressure.

7. Even a little exercise can make you think less anxiously. Studies have shown that any amount of exercise, from a brisk 10 minute walk to an intense aerobics or weightlifting session, seems to decrease feelings of anxiety.

尽管科研人员对此意见不一，但一份回顾过去多种研究的报告发现长期的锻炼，尤其是包括长时间、高强度训练阶段的训练，对抑郁症几乎同心理治疗一样有效。（当然，这并不是说你不应该求助于心理治疗。如果你觉得可能受抑郁症影响，首先应咨询心理健康专家。）

6. 锻炼能帮助人们适应工作、生活或其他方面的压力（可能因为锻炼本身也是一种压力），帮助调节身体来应付压力。澳大利亚研究人员对比每周三次做 30 分钟有氧健身操的人和练习渐进式放松技巧的人时发现：前一组人员更能适应高度紧张，血压更低。

7. 即使少量的锻炼也能减轻焦虑。研究表明：锻炼不论时间长短，从 10 分钟的健步行走到剧烈的有氧健身操或举重，似乎都能减少焦虑感。

8. 有氧锻炼可以使你的思维更加敏锐。日积月累，心脏锻炼（加上健康的饮食）会改善向大脑输送氧气和营养物质的血液质量。

9. 有规律的锻炼可以使你更聪明，降低随年龄增长大脑功能退化的可能性。最近伊利诺伊大学的动物实验表明：实际上锻炼能帮助大脑新细胞的产生。

10. 有几项研究表明：有规律地练习举重

❹ strenuous
/ˈstrenjʊəs/
adj. 必须努力的
❺ aerobic
/eəˈrəʊbɪk/
adj. 有氧的，耗氧的

8. Aerobic exercise may make you think better.Over time, cardio exercise (coupled with a healthful diet) improves the flow of blood that carries oxygen and nutrients[6] to your brain.

9. Working out regularly may make you smarter now and lessen the possibility that you'll lose brain function[7] as you age. According to a recent animal study at the University of Illinois, exercise can actually help the brain develop new cells.

10. In several studies, regular weight training or aerobic exercise was shown to improve the quality and duration of sleep. Naturally, this can make you less fatigued and be able to function better during the day.

11. Like meditation, hobbies or any other leisure activity, exercise gives your mind a needed break from everyday thoughts, responsibilities and commitments.

Finally, there's one more reason to keep exercising. When you work out regularly (but don't overstrain), your body simply functions better — you are better, healthier and less likely to suffer painful physical conditions. And that just plain feels good.

或有氧锻炼能改善睡眠质量，延长睡眠时间。这自然就会减少你的疲惫感，从而能在白天更好地工作。

11. 像静坐默想、个人嗜好或其他任何休闲活动一样，锻炼使你的大脑在日常思考、责任和负担之余得到必要的休息。

最后还有一条坚持锻炼的理由。当你有规律地进行锻炼（但不要过度）时，你的身体绝对运转得更好——你会更健壮、更健康，更少感到疼痛。那种感觉就是棒。

❻ nutrient
/ˈnjuːtrɪənt/
adj. 有营养的
❼ function
/ˈfʌŋkʃn/
v. 起作用

The history of chocolate

巧克力的历史

Spanish monks, who had been consigned to process the cocoa beans, finally let the secret out.

负责整个种植可可豆过程的西班牙修道士最终泄露了秘密。

American-made chocolate and cocoa products number in the hundreds. There is a fascinating[1] story behind these wonderful products. To tell that story and to provide a better understanding of the chocolate industry and its long-standing traditions is the purpose of this essay. The story of chocolate is essentially a layman's[2] introduction to the subject. It will provide readers an opportunity to view the industry as a whole.

Chocolate through the years

The story of chocolate, as far back as we know it, begins with the discovery of America. Until 1492, the Old World knew nothing at all about the delicious and stimulating flavor that was to become the favorite of millions.

The Court of King Ferdinand and Queen Isabella got its first look at the principal ingredient[3] of chocolate when Columbus returned in triumph from America and laid before the Spanish throne a treasure trove of many strange and wonderful things. Among these were a few dark brown beans that looked like almonds and seemed most unpromising. They were cocoa beans, today's source of all our chocolate and cocoa.

The King and Queen never dreamed how important cocoa beans could be, and it remained for Hernando Cortez, the great Spanish explorer, to grasp the commercial[4] possibilities of the New World offerings.

美国产的巧克力和可可产品有上百种，在这些美味的背后有一段迷人的故事。给你讲述这段历史并且让你更好地了解巧克力工业和悠久的传统是本文的目的。巧克力的历史实质上是一个非专业者对这个主题的介绍，这将给读者提供一个了解工业作为一个整体的机会。

走过岁月的巧克力

巧克力的历史，据我们所知，始于美洲的发现。直到1492年，旧世界的人才知道人世间居然有这种可口和沁人心脾的美味，而这美味早已成了千百万人的最爱。

斐迪南宫廷和伊莎贝拉女王第一次见到巧克力的主要成分时是哥伦布从美洲大陆凯旋而归，献给西班牙王族一个有许多稀奇玩艺的贵重发现物时。其中就有一种像宝石的深棕色的豆类，似乎没有什么太大用处。这些就是可可豆，也就是今天我们吃的巧克力和可可的来源。

国王和女王怎么也没想到小小的可可豆有多么重要，是伟大的西班牙探险家荷那多·科特，抓住了这个新世界提供的商机。

上帝的食物

在攻克墨西哥期间，科特发现印第安人用这些可可豆筹备王宫的饮品。"巧克力"，

❶ **fascinating**
/ˈfæsɪneɪtɪŋ/
adj. 迷人的，醉人的

❷ **layman**
/ˈleɪmən/
n. 外行人

❸ **ingredient**
/ɪnˈɡriːdɪənt/
n. 成分，原料，要素

❹ **commercial**
/kəˈmɜːʃl/
adj. 商业的

Food of the Gods

During his conquest of Mexico, Cortez found the Aztec Indians using cocoa beans in the preparation of the royal drink of the realm, "chocolate," meaning warm liquid. In 1519, Emperor Montezuma, who reportedly drank 50 or more portions daily, served chocolate to his Spanish guests in great golden goblets, treating it like a food for the gods.

For all its regal importance, however, Montezuma's chocolate was very bitter, and the Spaniards did not find it to their taste. To make the concoction more agreeable to Europeans, Cortez and his countrymen conceived the idea of sweetening it with cane sugar.

While they took chocolate back to Spain, the idea found favor and the drink underwent several more changes with newly discovered spices[5], such as cinnamon and vanilla. Ultimately, someone decided the drink would taste better if served hot.

The new drink quickly won friends, especially among the Spanish aristocracy.

Spain wisely proceeded to plant cacao in its overseas colonies, which gave birth to a very profitable business. Remarkably enough, the Spanish succeeded in keeping the art of the cocoa industry a secret from the rest of Europe for nearly a hundred years.

Chocolate spreads to Europe

Spanish monks, who had been consigned to process the co-

意思是暖和的液体。在 1519 年，蒙特祖马皇帝把巧克力放在一个大的金制高脚杯里，款待他的西班牙客人，对待巧克力俨然像为上帝准备的食物一样，据说这个皇帝每天喝 50 甚至更多份巧克力。

尽管巧克力有帝王气派，蒙特祖马的巧克力却非常苦，并不合西班人的口味，为了把它调制得更加适合欧洲人的口味，科特和他的同胞们产生了加糖把它变甜的想法。

当他们把巧克力带回西班牙的时候，这个想法获得了许多人的赞同，而且巧克力也经历了新变化，诸如加入新发现的桂皮和香草等调味品。最后，有人认为如果把巧克力煮热了喝口感会更好。

这种新饮品很快受到了欢迎，尤其在西班牙贵族阶层，西班牙明智地做出了在海外殖民地种植可可的决定，也就诞生了一个赚钱的行业。

很显然，在近 100 多年，对于其他欧洲人来说，西班牙成功经营可可工业一直是个秘密。

巧克力风靡欧洲

负责整个种植可可豆过程的西班牙修道士最终泄露了秘密，不久，巧克力便风靡欧洲成了一种美味健康的食品，巧克力还一度

❺ **spice** /spaɪs/
n. 调料；香味；调味品

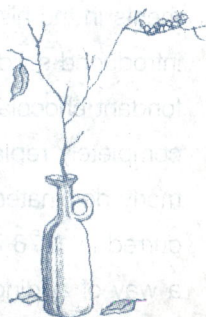

coa beans, finally let the secret out. It did not take long before chocolate was acclaimed throughout Europe as a delicious, health-giving food. For a while it reigned as the drink at the fashionable Court of France. Chocolate drinking spread across the Channel to Great Britain, and in 1657 the first of many famous English Chocolate Houses appeared.

The hand methods of manufacture used by small shops gave way in time to the mass production of chocolate. The transition was hastened by the advent of a perfected steam engine, which mechanized the cocoa grinding process. By 1730, chocolate had dropped in price from three dollars or more per pound to within financial reach of all. The invention of the cocoa press in 1828 reduced the prices even further and helped to improve the quality of the beverage by squeezing out part of the cocoa butter, the fat that occurs naturally in cocoa beans. From then on, drinking chocolate had more of the smooth consistency and the pleasing flavor it has today.

The 19th Century marked two more revolutionary developments in the history of chocolate. In 1847, an English company introduced solid "eating chocolate" through the development of fondant chocolate, a smooth and velvety variety that has almost completely replaced the old coarse grained chocolate which formerly dominated[6] the world market. The second development occurred in 1876 in Vevey, Switzerland, when Daniel Peter devised a way of adding milk to the chocolate, creating the product we enjoy today known as milk chocolate.

成为时尚的法国宫廷的主要饮品，巧克力通过海峡传到了英国，1657年第一批著名的英国巧克力公司诞生了。

　　大批量的生产最终取代了小型的手工生产。蒸汽动力的出现加速了这个转变过程，蒸汽动力使碾碎可可豆的过程机械化了，在1730年，巧克力的价格从3美元或3美元多一磅降到了大众价，1828年巧克力压缩机的出现进一步导致巧克力价格的下降，同时也通过挤出巧克力内的部分黄油而改善了饮料的质量，这部分油脂存在于可可豆中。从那时起，饮用巧克力饮料的习惯一直持续至今，它那令人愉悦的口味也延续至今。

　　巧克力的历史在19世纪经历了两次革命性的大发展。1847年，一家英国公司通过开发巧克力发明了"固体巧克力"，这种柔软光滑的品种几乎完全取代了曾一度主宰世界市场的粗糙磨压的巧克力，第二次发展是1876年在瑞士思威，凡尼尔·彼得发明了一种在巧克力中加入牛奶的方法，因而创造了至今仍受人们喜爱牛奶巧克力。

巧克力亮相美国

　　在美国，巧克力的生产以领先于世界的速度发展着。这是在1765年新英格兰革命之前，确切地说，第一家巧克力工厂就诞生在这个国

❻ dominate
/ˈdɒmɪneɪt/
v. 支配；统治

Chocolate comes to America

In the United States of America, the production of chocolate proceeded at a faster pace than anywhere else in the world. It was in pre-Revolutionary New England — 1765, to be exact — that the first chocolate factory was established in this country.

Chocolate has gained so much importance since that time that any interruption in its supply would be keenly felt.

During World War II, the U.S. government recognized chocolate's role in the nourishment and group spirit of the Allied Armed Forces, so much so that it allocated valuable shipping space for the importation of cocoa beans. Many soldiers were thankful for the pocket chocolate bars which gave them the strength to carry on until more food rations[7] could be obtained. Today, the U.S. Army D-rations include three 4-ounce chocolate bars. Chocolate has even been taken into space as part of the diet of U.S. astronauts.

家。

　　从那时起，巧克力的重要性就变得非同寻常了，以致供应上的任何阻断都变得异常敏感。

　　在第二次世界大战期间，美国政府意识到了巧克力在营养和培养空军团队精神中的重要性，于是为进口可可豆提供了广阔的运输空间，许多士兵都感谢他们口袋中的巧克力棒，因为有了它，他们才能坚持到有粮食吃的那一天。今天，美国军队的口粮中还包括4盎司的巧克力。巧克力甚至作为美国宇航员食物的一部分被带到太空中。

❼ ration /'ræʃn/
n. 定量，配给限额

The joy of SOHO: making a life while making a living

SOHO一族的快乐：生存与生活

You will have the freedom to enjoy the profits of your own work, and the continuing growth and profit which comes from owning your own business.

你会有充分的自由，享受成功带来的快乐，也可以享受拥有自己的事业并使其不断发展赢利给你带来的快乐。

A better choice

The next time you overhear[1] a friend or coworker chattering excitedly about SOHO, don't assume[2] that they are talking about New York. In today's business world SOHO refers to "Small Office/Home Office," one of today's biggest explosions in the economy. The home-based business has been born out of necessity. In an era when large corporations always think of downsizing[3], what are your other choices?

Your choices are usually limited: find a lucrative niche in the small business world, stand in line at Unemployment, or accept a cut in pay and benefits. We were all raised to give 9 hours work for 8 hours pay, and we are not backing away from that. Bosses don't understand that you just put braces on your child's teeth and now have to pay for them. In this economic climate, where cost-cutting measures are the group of the day, setting up a home office on your own may just be the ticket to beat the odds. So now, to configure your own small office, home office set-up can be a breeze.

How to start

Let's congratulate on your decision to start your own business. But where do you go from here? Paper clips, memo pad, phone and table? Almost but not quite. One of the faults committed by home-based business owners otherwise known as a small office home office is that they fail to consider the possibilities of expansion.

一个不错的选择

下次当你无意中听到一个朋友或同事兴致勃勃地谈论 SOHO 时，不要认为他们在谈论纽约，在今天这个商业世界中 SOHO 是指"小型办公室／家庭办公室"，是今日经济的最大爆点之一。以家庭为基础的生意已经应运而生了，在这个大公司不断考虑裁员的时代，你还有其他的选择吗？

你的选择通常是有限制的：在小生意世界中找到一个赚钱的位置，加入失业大军或接受减薪薄利。我们工作 9 小时却得到 8 小时的报酬，既便这样我们也没有后退，老板们并不理解你只是给你的孩子安了个牙套，现在你却得拿出钞票付款，在经济大环境下，低成本的措施已成为大小集团的首要选择，在家里建一个你自己的办公室无疑是在竞争中脱颖而出的法宝。所以，赶快设计一个你自己的小型办公室，家庭办公室真的是这个商业天地的一缕清风。

怎样起步

首先祝贺你决定开创你自己的事业了，但从哪开始做起呢？文件夹、记事薄、电话和办公桌？差不多了但还不是全部，开展家庭办公的创业者的一个不成熟的地方是他们没有考虑扩展的可能性。

---

❶ overhear

/ˌeʊvəˈhɪə/

v. 无意中听到

❷ assume

/əˈsjuːm/

v. 假定，假设

❸ downsize

/ˈdaʊnsaɪz/

v. 裁员

It is fine to start working from the kitchen table but what happens when things start to take off and you still do not want to have an office space? Where do you place the home office? If you have the space, I highly suggest a room unto itself. This permits you to close the door and separate your personal life from business. You are able to leave everything you are working on right where it is instead of shaving to clean-up for dinner or to go to bed. These clean-up steps can lead to problems down the road. Where you anchor the home office is important for your future success. A corner in the living room, bedroom or attic is preferable if you do not have a room solely for your business. Reasons for the separation include fewer distractions and the ability to think and focus more clearly.

And you may have to have one or two clients come to your "office" in the lifetime of your business. Even though it is your home, you want to present the best professional atmosphere possible, which is very important if you have people working with you. Their productivity is important to your bottom line. Invest in the appropriate chairs, tables, lighting and ventilation[4] before you invest in the paper clips and the stapler. If you are not comfortable, neither you nor your employees will stay there and finish the job. Bottom line: Your employees don't want to interact or become a part of your family issues. It is fine to have employees in your home but just make sure you supply them with the best working atmosphere possible.

　　在餐桌上开始工作没什么不好的，但当你的事业逐步发展可你不想拥有一个办公空间，事情会变得怎样呢？你要在哪儿建一个家庭办公室呢？如果空间够大，我建议你建立独立的办公空间，这样你就可以关上门，把事业和私人生活空间分开了。你就可以让一切照旧保持原样，可以不必收拾办公用品腾出地方吃饭或睡觉了。这些整理步聚可以清除事业发展上的障碍，一个家庭办公室的开创对你未来的成功是非常重要的，如果你没有单独的空间可以利用，那起居室、卧室的一个角落或阁楼也不失为不错的选择，因为这样的隔离不会有很多的干扰，可以更加清醒专心地考虑问题。

　　在你的事业中，或许会有一两个客户光顾你的"办公室"，既使是在家里，你也要尽可能创造出最好的职业氛围，如果你想有人与你共同奋斗这是非常重要的。他们的创作力对于你的成功底线至关重要，在投资文件夹和钉书机前先在合适的桌椅、光线和通风方面上投资一下吧，如果没有令人舒适的环境，你和你的雇员都不会留下来完成工作。成功底线：你的雇员既不想干涉你的家庭事务也不想成为你家庭生活中的一部分。让雇员在你的家里工作这很好，但要保证给他们

❹ ventilation
/ˌventɪˈleɪʃn/
n. 通风；换气

The popularity of being SOHO

Today, researchers and marketers have identified a segment that is now labeled SOHO, small offices, home offices, whether they are high-tech start-ups or women selling Mary Kay. But they drive America's economic growth and have created most of the new jobs in the last 20 years. 3% of companies accounted for 6 million of the 7.7 million jobs that were added to the economy between 1991—1995. Small businesses represent over 90% of all businesses in the U.S. with an economic output greater than Germany or France or the UK.

Reportedly, home-based workers earn more money. The 46 million home-based workers in the United States, including a large number of women, working at home in an attempt to better balance work and family, earn 28% more than the average office worker, and spend less time making their pay. Of course this could be due, in part, to the fact that more experienced and aggressive[5] workers tend to start their own businesses.

Remember, going into business on your own, or from a home office may mean making do with less. But it can also mean achieving more: more independence, more challenges, more results. In the long run it may well mean more money for you and your family. In a word, doing it on your own means freedom, to grow, experiment and learn. If you are successful, you won't have to go ask for a raise or accept what you're given or worry about being turned out to pasture when a younger version of yourself comes along. You will have the freedom to enjoy the prof-

尽可能提供最好的工作氛围。

有多少 SOHO 族

今天，研究员和市场调查员确定了可称之为 SOHO 族的范围，小型办公室、家庭办公室，无论他们是高科技创业还是销售妇女美莲凯品牌……但他们推动着美国经济的发展而且在过去 20 年里大多数新的工作职位都是他们创造的，在 1991 至 1995 年间，770万出现在经济中的新工作中有 6 百万是由3%的公司创造的，在美国小公司代表了美国所有公司的 90%，它们的经济产量超过德国、法国或是英国。

据报道，以家庭为主的工人赚的钱更多，在美国 4 600 万的 SOHO 族（包括相当多的妇女），在家工作以期望较好地平衡工作与家庭的关系，他们比一般的办公室白领多赚20%，而且工作时间也相对较少，当然了，在一定程度上说，只有那些经验丰富且雄心勃勃的工人倾向于建立他们自己的事业。

记住，开创你自己的事业或建立一个家庭工作室或许意味着你要学会凑合。但同时也意味着你会得到更多：更多独立、更多挑战、更多成就。从长远的角度看，这也意味着你可以为你和你的家庭赚更多钱，总之一句话，自己开创事业意味着自由、成长、体

⑤ aggressive
/əˈgresɪv/
adj. 有进取心的，好斗的

its[6] of your own work， and the continuing growth and profit which comes from owning your own business. Good luck and enjoy the journey.

验和学习，如果你成功了，你就不必要求加薪，或者接受你现在的薪水，也不必因为出现像你一样的年轻人而担忧了。你会有充分的自由，享受成功带来的快乐，也可以享受拥有自己的事业不断发展给你带来的快乐。祝你好运，并享受旅程。

❻ profit /ˈprɒfɪt/
n. 利润；利益

What is a great book?

什么样的书堪称
伟大作品？

A great book need not even be a best seller in its own day. It may take time for it to accumulate its ultimate audience.

一本名著并非只在它自己的时代畅销不衰，它可能会随时间的推移拥有越来越多的读者。

There is no end to the making of books. Nor does there seem to be any end to the making of lists of "great books." There have always been more books than anyone could read. And as they have multiplied[1] through the centuries, more and more blue-ribbon lists have had to be made.

No matter how long your life, you will, at best, be able to read only a few books of all that have been written, and the few you do read should include the best. You can rejoice[2] in the fact that the number of such is relatively small.

What are the signs by which we may recognize a great book? The six mentioned below may not be all there are, but they are the ones which are found most useful in explaining the choices over the years.

Great books are probably the most widely read. They are not best sellers for a year or two. They are enduring best sellers. *Gone with the wind* has had relatively few readers compared to the plays of Shakespeare or *Don Quixote*. It would be reasonable to estimate that Homer's *Iliad* has been read by at least 25,000,000 people in the last 3000 years.

A great book need not even be a best seller in its own day. It may take time for it to accumulate its ultimate[3] audience. The astronomer Kepler, whose work on the planetary motions is now a classic, is reported to have said of his book that "it may wait a century for a reader, as God has waited 6000 years for an observer."

各种书的诞生是永无止境的，似乎出现在"伟大作品"榜上的书永无止境。总有读不完的书，一个世纪又一个世纪的积累，越来越多的优秀书榜上有名。

无论你的生命历程有多长，最多你只能阅读所有书中的一部分，而你所读的这些书里应该包括最好的，你会为这样相对小的数目感到高兴。

什么样的书才能称得上是伟大作品呢？以下提到的几点虽算不上面面俱到，但它们确是多年来我们选择的最好解释。

一本伟大作品可能是被最广为阅读的书。它们不仅是一两年的畅销书，相反它们的受欢迎程度是经久不衰的。与莎士比亚或唐吉诃德比起来，《飘》相对拥有较少的读者，荷马的《伊利亚特》在过去的 3,000 年间曾有 2,500 万读者，得出这样的估计是完全合理的。

一本名著并非只在它自己的时代畅销不衰，它可能会随时间的推移拥有越来越多的读者。有报道说天文学家克卜勒曾说过他的书"会等待一个世纪迎来一个读者，就像上帝等待 6,000 年迎来一个观察者一样"。克卜勒的关于行星运动的著作现在成了一部经典著作。

❶ **multiply**
/ˈmʌltəˌplaɪ/
n. 增加；增值

❷ **rejoice**
/rɪˈdʒɔɪs/
v. 感到高兴，充满喜悦

❸ **ultimate**
/ˈʌltəmɪt/
adj. 最后的，最终的

Great books are the most readable. They will not let you down if you try to read them well. They have more ideas per page than most books have in their entirety[4]. That is why you can read a great book over and over again and never exhaust its contents.

They can be read at many different levels of understanding, as well as with a great diversity of interpretations. Obvious examples are ROBINSON CRUSOE and the ODYSSEY. Children can read them with enjoyment, but fail to find therein all the beauty and significance, which delight an adult mind.

Great books are the most instructive. This follows from the fact that they are original communications; they contain what cannot be found it other books. Whether you ultimately agree or disagree with what they say, these are the primary teachers of mankind; they have made the basic contributions to human thought.

It is almost unnecessary to add that the great books are the most influential books. In the tradition of learning, they have been most discussed by readers who have also been writers. These are the books about which there are many other books — countless and, for the most part, forgotten.

Great books deal with the persistently[5] unsolved problems of human life. There are genuine mysteries in the world that mark the limits of human knowing and thinking. Inquiry not only begins with wonder, but usually ends with it also. Great minds acknowledge mysteries honestly. Wisdom is fortified not destroyed, by under

伟大作品是最适合阅读的，如果你用心地读，它们是不会让你失望的，它们每一页所包含的思想都多于其它大多数书包含的全部思想。这就是为什么你读了伟大作品一遍又一遍，但每次都有新东西的原因了。

著作适于不同理解层次的人阅读，同样也可以有不同的解释，因人而异。像鲁滨逊和奥德赛都是很明显的例子。孩子们能津津有味地读，但却体会不到那些取悦成年人思想的美感和价值感。

伟大作品是最有教育意义的。这是因为它们在最初就是具有交流目的，它们包含其他书里所没有的宝藏。无论你最终是否同意书中的思想内容，它们始终是人类主要的老师，是人类思想的基本贡献因素。

再补充说伟大作品是最有影响的书几乎就没有必要了。在传统的学术知识界，通常评论伟大作品最多的读者自己本身也是作家，他们的书写的是关于那些尽管不计其数却多数被遗忘。

伟大作品著作是一直在关注人类社会那些尚无法解决的问题，在这个标记着人类认知极深的世界上确定有一些真正神秘的东西，疑问经常源于好奇，却也通常以好奇告终。大思想想家们从内心里是承认神秘的存在的。

❹ **entirety**
/inˈtaɪərətɪ/
n. 完全，全部

❺ **persistently**
/pəˈsɪstəntlɪ/
adv. 持续地，一直地

standing its limitations.

It is our privilege[6], as readers, to belong to the larger brotherhood of man which recognizes no national boundaries. I do not know how to escape from the strait-jacket of political nationalism. I do know how we become friends of the human spirit in all its manifestations[7], regardless of time and place. It is by reading the great books.

通过理解智慧的极限得到了加强，而不是遭到了毁灭。

能属于这个没有国界的大家族，这是我们作为读者的荣幸。我不知道怎样摆脱政治民族主义的束缚，但我却明白无论时空怎么变化，我们是如何成为精神的各个方面的朋友的。这就是通过阅读著作。

❻ privilege
/ˈprɪvlɪdʒ/
n./v. 特权，基本人权；给予特权

❼ manifestation
/ˌmænɪfeˈsteɪʃn/
n. 表现

A once-and-for-all splurge[1]

一生一次的炫耀

The 28-year-old is finally ending his bachelor-hood. Also coming to an end are his bank savings, accumulated over the years.

28岁的他终于要结束单身生活了，而与此同时他多年来在银行的存款也要所剩无几了。

The approaching[2] National Day Holiday is going to be special for Jason Li.

The 28-year-old is finally ending his bachelorhood. Also coming to an end are his bank savings, accumulated over the years.

"I had never thought marrying would be so dear," Li said.

The studio wedding photos alone cost him 5,000 yuan. "But it is indispensable, as my fiancée firmly believes that a woman becomes most beautiful when she wears the wedding gown, so that moment must be captured and kept forever." Li said, forcing a smile.

The price tag

Both Li and his future wife are from traditional families, which determine that a lavish wedding banquet[3] is a must.

Li chose the three-star New Garden Hotel to hold the grand feast. Taking all the necessary guests, including relatives, colleagues[4], friends and former classmatess into account, Li found that they have a total of 250 guests. That is 25 tables.

"When the restaurant showed me the final price after several rounds of bargaining — 35,000 yuan, I couldn't help drawing a cold breath," Li said.

There is still much other expenditure[5] involved in the wedding

即将到来的国庆节对于 Jason Li 来说非同一般。

28 岁的他终于要结束单身生活了，而与此同时他多年来在银行的存款也要所剩无几了。

"我从来没想到结婚要花费这么多。"李说。

拍结婚照就花了他 5,000 元。"这也是必需的，因为我的未婚妻坚信女人穿上婚纱时最漂亮。所以那一刻应该永久地保存下来。"李说道，勉强挤出一丝笑容来。

价目单

李和她的未婚妻都来自传统家庭，两家都坚定地认为举办一场豪华的婚礼是必不可少的。

李选择了在三星级新花园酒店举办他们的婚礼。李算了一下所有要参加婚礼的客人数目，包括亲戚、同事、朋友还有以前的同学，总共有 250 人。

"几番还价之后，饭店老板让我看最后的价格时（3.5 万），我不禁倒吸一口冷气。"李说。

婚礼上还有许多其它的花费：要发的烟糖 6,000 元，还有拍照，录像 600 元。

❶ splurge
/splɜ:dʒ/
n. 炫耀

❷ approaching
/əˈprəʊtʃɪŋ/
adj. 邻近的

❸ banquet
/ˈbæŋkwɪt/
n. 宴会，酒会

❹ colleague
/ˈkɒli:g/
n. 同事

❺ expenditure
/ɪkˈspendɪtʃə/
n. 花费，花销

ceremony. A rough account for the sweets and cigarettes to be handed out at the wedding party is about 6,000 yuan, plus a further 600 yuan for photographs and a video recording.

The rent of suits to be worn at the wedding party (two dresses for the bride and one for the groom) is 300 yuan. "She still bought a 3,000 yuan wedding gown," Li added.

Renting the car and then decorating the car with flowers and hiring a make-up girl for the bride, all these take money.

Li figures out that the overall cost of the wedding ceremony is at least 60,000 yuan. Earning 2,500 yuan a month, Li has withdrawn all his savings for the big day.

The general trend

A survey of some 300 newlyweds[6] showed that over 80 percent of the couples were prepared to spend around 60,000 yuan on the wedding. About 5-8 per cent of people would spend more than that, and this percentage is steadily rising.

The five-star hotel's so-called super luxurious wedding banquet of 588 yuan per person plus 15 per cent surcharge is fully booked, despite the fact that at least 10 tables must be reserved.

What luxury entails[7]

For those who are determined to hold an impressive wedding

租来的结婚礼服 300 元（新娘新郎各一套）。她还买了一套 3,000 元的婚纱呢。"李补充说。

还要租车，然后装饰，给新娘请化妆师，这都得花钱啊！

李算了算，整个婚礼要花去 6 万元，每月只有 2,500 元工资的李为了这一天花掉了他所有的积蓄。

流行趋势

对 300 对即将结婚的男女所作的一项调查显示，80%以上的人准备为他们的婚礼花费 60,000 元，大约 5%到 8%的人愿意花更多，而且这个数目正在持续稳定增长。

五星级酒店所谓的超豪华婚宴（每人 588 元加上 15% 的额外费用）总是被全部预定，尽管要求是预定数目最少不低于 10 桌。

奢华需要付出多少

对于那些决心办一场令人难忘的婚礼的人来说，婚宴就不能仅仅限于吃喝的层次上了。

婚宴上需要有乐队来使气氛活跃起来，要有一位有经验的婚礼主持人让仪式顺利进行，要有无数玫瑰鲜花为婚礼增加浪漫情调。这意味着 6,000 元的额外开支。

这和 70 年代改革开放以前比起来大相径

❻ newlyweds
/'nju:lɪwedz/
n. 新婚夫妇

ceremony, the party can't be limited to just eating and drinking.

It also requires a band to play up the atmosphere, an experienced host to make the whole ceremony smooth, and numerous roses to add more romance to the party, which means extra costs of at least 6,000 yuan.

This is all a radical change from the pre-economic reform period of the 1970s when restaurants were rarely mentioned when talking about weddings, let alone five-star hotels or bands. Wedding banquets were mostly held at the couple's own home, and dishes were prepared by parents and close relatives.

If account is taken of the new apartment, house appliances and the honeymoon, all of which have now been included among the city's new marriage essentials, the cost of getting married is really tremendous[7].

Who pays the bill?

Compared with 20 years ago, when a couple amassed a bicycle, a radio and some furniture then had their union rubber-stamped at a local government office, the changes are great.

Although many young people find spending too much on the wedding is actually unnecessary, most of them are also finding it hard to resist.

Part of the pressure comes from the parents. Over 95 percent

庭，那个时候人们结婚很少想到去饭店，更不用说五星级的酒店或乐队了。婚宴经常在双方家里举行，饭菜由父母亲戚帮忙来做就行了。

如果把已经成为现在新婚必不可少的新居，家电，蜜月都算上，结婚的确是一笔很大的开销。

谁来付账

相比之下，20 年前人们结婚时，攒够一辆自行车，半导体，一些家具，然后双方去当地政府登记盖章就好了。变化太大了。

虽然许多年轻人觉得实际上没有必要在婚礼上花费过多，但是大部分人也感觉到这个趋势很难抗拒。

一部分压力来自父母，有超过 90% 的父母坚决认为应该举办一场有几百位客人参加的体面的婚礼。

一些新奇的观点比如"旅行结婚"，意思是省钱度一个长时间的蜜月。虽然符合年轻人的口味，却遭到了父母的坚决反对。

也有来自同事的压力。当越来越多的年轻人极力办一场奢侈的婚礼时，新婚夫妇的婚礼如果过于简单难免觉得很尴尬。

❼ **tremendous**
/trɪˈmendəs/
adj. 极大的，巨大的

of parents strongly support the idea of a lavish[8] wedding ceremony involving several hundred guests.

Novel ideas such as a "travelling wedding", which saves money for the prolonged honeymoon, although agreeable to the young, are firmly objected to by their parents.

Then there is peer pressure. When more and more young people are striving for a luxurious wedding ceremony, it is easy for the newlyweds to feel embarrassed if their wedding is too simple.

Statistics show that last year the country's overall marriage-related expenditures reached 150 billion yuan, ranking it top among all types of domestic spending.

有统计显示，去年全国的有关结婚的总开支达 150 亿，居各种家庭开支之首。

❽ **lavish**

/ˈlævɪʃ/

adj. 浪费的，滥用的

The art of living

生活的艺术

A man comes to this world with his fist clenched, but when he dies, his hand is open.

人来到世上的时候，他的拳头是紧握着的，但当他离开的时候，他的手就松开了。

The art of living is to know when to hold fast and when to let go. For life is a paradox[1]: it enjoins us to cling to its many gifts even while it ordains their eventual relinquishment. The rabbis of old put it this way: "A man comes to this world with his fist clenched[2], but when he dies, his hand is open."

Surely we ought to hold fast to life, for it is wondrous, and full of a beauty that breaks through every pore of God's own earth. We know that this is so, but all too often we recognize this truth only in our backward glance when we remember what was and then suddenly realize that it is no more.

We remember a beauty that faded[3], a love that waned. But we remember with far greater pain that we did not see that beauty when it flowered, that we failed to respond with love when it was tendered.

A recent experience re-taught me this truth. I was hospital-ized following a severe heart attack and had been in intensive care for several days. It was not a pleasant place.

One morning, I had to have some additional tests. The re-quired machines were located in a building at the opposite end of the hospital, so I had to be wheeled across the courtyard on a gurney.

As we emerged from our unit, the sunlight hit me. That's all there was to my experience. Just the light of the sun. And yet how

生活的艺术就在于你要知道什么时候要执着什么时候要放弃，因为生活就是矛盾：它赏赐我们所有美好的东西又最终全部收回。正如一位古代的先生所说："人来到世上的时候，他的拳头足紧握着的，但当他离开的时候，他的手就松开了。"

我们当然应该对生活坚守执着，因为生活是神奇的，到处可见上帝赐予我们的美丽，我们知道生活是如此美丽的，但只有当我们最后看它一眼知道它将失去的时候才感受到这个事实。

我们会记得美丽削损，爱情远去的时候，但当我们想起在花朵绽放的时候没有欣赏它在爱情包围的时候没有珍惜它的时候，我们会更加痛苦。

最近的一次经历又让我认识到了这个真理，在一次严重的心脏突发后，我住院了，在特护病房住了几天，这可不是一个让人愉快的地方。

一天早上，我需要附加检验了，检测仪器在医院尽头的对面，因此我必须躺在盖尼式轮椅上被推着穿过医院。

当我们出现在院里时，阳光洒在了我身上。这就是我那时的感受，仅仅是一片阳光，多么美丽啊——暖融融的，亮晶晶的，光芒

❶ paradox
/ˈpærədɒks/
n. 自相矛盾，荒谬说法

❷ clench
/klentʃ/
v. 咬紧（牙关），握紧（拳头）

❸ fade
/feɪd/
vi. 退色，失去光泽

beautiful it was — how warming, how sparking, how brilliant! I looked to see whether anyone else relished the sun's golden glow, but everyone was hurrying to and fro, most with eyes fixed on the ground. Then I remembered how often I, too, had been indifferent to the grandeur of each day, too preoccupied with petty and sometimes even mean concerns to respond from that experience is really as commonplace as was the experience itself: life's gifts are precious — but we are too heedless of them.

Here then is the first pole of life's paradoxical demands on us: Never too busy for the wonder and the awe of life. Be reverent before each dawning day. Embrace each hour. Seize each golden minute.

Hold fast to life, but not so fast that you cannot let go. This is the second side of life's coin, the opposite pole of its paradox: we must accept our losses, and learn how to let go.

This is not an easy lesson to learn, especially when we are young and think that the world is ours to command, that whatever we desire with the full force of our passionate[4] being can, nay, will, be ours. But then life moves along to confront us with realities, and slowly but surely this truth dawns upon us.

At every stage of life we sustain losses — and grow in the process. We begin our independent lives only when we emerge from the womb and lose its protective shelter. We enter a progression of schools, then we leave our mothers and fathers and

四射的！我四处张望看是否也有其他人享受
太阳的光辉，但每个人都来去匆匆，大部分
人两眼直直地盯着地面，这使我想起我自己
对每天的光芒也一直熟视无睹。太在乎日常
琐事，而忘了去发现身边的美丽，这种体验
也正在他们现在的作法一样，是那么可认为
常：生活的礼物是宝贵的，但我们却看不到
它们。

　　这就是生活的矛盾给我们的第一个启迪：
放慢脚步欣赏生活的点滴。用一颗虔诚的心
迎接清晨的曙光，拥抱每一小时，分秒必争。

　　空守一份执着，但不要太执着，该放手
的时候就要放手。这是人生"硬币"的另一
面，也就是矛盾的另一面：我们必须接受失
去所拥有的，并且学会放弃。

　　但这样的训诫是不容易学会的，尤其在
我们年青的时候，我们认为世界尽在我们的
掌握中，只要我们有满腔热情，无论我们渴
望什么都会得到的，但是当生活让我们尝到
了现实的滋味时，我们才慢慢明白这个道理。

　　在生命的每个阶段，我们都要忍受失去
一些东西，而且在这个过程中成长。从我们
出生的那一刻起，我们开始了独立的生活，
我们上了小学、中学然后上大学，然后离开
父母和我们童年的家，我们结婚生子，然后

4 passionate
/ˈpæʃənət/
n. 热情的，多情的

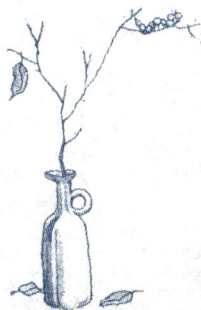

our childhood homes. We get married and have children and then have to let them go. We confront the death of our parents and our spouses. We face the gradual or not so gradual waning of our strength. And ultimately, as the parable of the open and closed hand suggests, we must confront the inevitability of our own demise[5], losing ourselves as it were, all that we were or dreamed to be.

又看着我们的孩子离开我们，我们要面对父母和伴侣终有一天会离我们而去，我们面对自我日渐地衰老，最后，正像那个紧握和松开手的寓言所暗示的，我们必须最终面对自己从人世间消失，失去所有的一切，无论是曾拥有的还是梦想拥有的，我们最终会两手空空地离开人世。

❺ demise
/dɪˈmaɪz/
n. 死亡

Let go

放 手

This is what happens in life. The more you are able to let go and flow with life, the more life takes care of itself.

这就是生活，你越能坦然地面对一切，顺其自然，命运越能帮助走好人生。

The experience of love is an inner state. When this is present, you are happy, alive, and free. You feel good about yourself and good about life. As you bring the experience of love into your life, life works effortlessly[1] and great things happen.

The opposite of love is fear and upset. When this is present, you lose down inside. You lose your creativity[2] and your ability to see clearly. You get tunnel vision and you interact in a way that almost always makes your situation worse.

Whether you live in a state of love or a state of upset depends, not on your circumstances, but on how you relate to your circumstances. A good way to see this is to look at upsets.

Upsets seem to be caused by what happens but they're not. Upsets are caused by your fighting and resisting what happens. To see this in your life, select a recent upset. Now notice what would happen if somehow you were at peace with what happened. There would be no upset.

There would be no upset because upsets aren't caused by what happened. Upsets are caused by fighting and resisting what happened. The moment you take away the fighting and resisting, the upset disappears[3].

To live the experience of love, and to create a life that works, you need to stop the fighting and resisting. You do this through a process called letting go.

　　爱的体验是一种心理状态，当爱来临的时候，你感到幸福，充满生机，感到自由，你对自己充满信心，觉得生活是美好的，当你把这种爱的体验带进生活中时，生活就变得轻松了，美好的事就随处可见了。

　　爱的反面是恐惧和不安。当恐惧和不安困扰你的时候，你的心情就不再平静了，你失去了创造力和洞察世间万物的能力，你视野狭窄，总将事情弄得一塌糊涂。

　　你生活在爱的海洋还是烦恼的天地其实不是取决于你的环境，而是取决于你处理环境的方式。一个不错的方法就是看着你的烦恼。

　　烦恼似乎是由所发生的事引起的，其实不然。烦恼来源于你对现实的对抗与抵制。为了证实生活中的这一点，挑一件最近的烦心事分析一下。现在试一下如果你坦然面对生活中的苦乐是非，看看会怎样，根本就不会有烦恼。

　　其实是没有烦恼的。因为烦恼不是所发生的事带来的。它是因为你对抗和抵制事实。当你不再对抗和抵制它，烦恼就消失了。

　　为了生活中充满爱，也为了创造一种充实高效的生活，你需要停止对抗与抵制。为此你要经历一个过程——放手。

❶ effortlessly
/ˈefətlɪslɪ/
adv. 不遗余力地
❷ creativity
/ˌkriːeɪˈtɪvətɪ/
n. 创造力
❸ disappear
/ˌdɪsəˈpɪə/
v. 消失

Letting go is the inner action that releases the fear and upset. The moment you let go, everything seems to change. With the fear and upset gone, you see your situation very differently.

You become creative and discover solutions that you could never have seen before.

To let go, you need to do the opposite of fighting and resisting. You need to let go of your demands and expectations for how life should be and make peace with the way life is.

Find what you are resisting. Then give it full permission to be there. If you have a fear of losing a relationship, be willing to be it. If you are resisting the way someone is, then give the person full permission to be that way.

Be willing for anything. Set yourself free inside. Then take whatever action you need to have your life be great.

Keep in mind that letting go is a state of mind and has nothing to do with your actions. Letting go is the process that removes the fear and upset so you can see what action you need to take.

In your heart, you can be willing to lose someone, but in your actions, do everything you can to make sure the person feels so loved that he or she would never want to leave.

To make letting go a little easier, there are several steps you

　　放手是一种心理活动，它能驱散恐惧和不安。从你决定放手，让世事顺其自然的那一刻开始，一切就开始变得不同了，随着恐惧与不安烟消云散，你就能以另一种角色看你的环境了。

　　人的头脑充满创造力，能够发现你以前怎么也想不到的解决问题的方法。

　　要放手，你需要走到对抗与抵制的对岸，你需要放弃你施加给生活的需求与期望，学会平静地对待生活。

　　找到你所抵制的东西是什么，然后给它开绿灯。如果你害怕失去一种关系，那就调整心态去面对吧，如果你抵制某人的行为方式，那就让他那么做吧，别管他。

　　心甘情愿接受任何事，在内心深处解放你自己，然后采取行动让你的生活变得充满阳光，记住放手是一种内心的状态，它与你采取的行动无关，放手是一种过程，它可以赶走恐惧与不安，让你清醒地看清下一步该怎么做。

　　在你心灵深处，你可以接受失去某人，但在行动上，你要尽一切力量使他或她感到情深意重而不愿离开。

　　为了让你能轻松地学会放手，你需要按下面的步聚去做。首先是相信，无论发生什

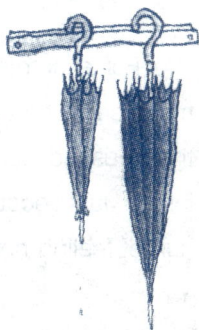

can take. The first is trusting. Trust that no matter what happens, you will be okay. When you know that you will be okay, letting go becomes relatively easy.

Trusting is also telling the truth. You really will be okay no matter what happens. Life is only threatening when you resist. So stop resisting and trust. Trust that no matter what happens, you will be okay.

The second step in the process of letting go is to be willing to feel your hurt. Be willing to feel all the hurt and the feelings of being not okay that your circumstances reactivate. Be willing to feel the hurt of being worthless[4] or not 'good enough.'

The avoidance of this hurt is what makes you resist. Once you are willing to feel this hurt, the need to resist disappears. You can then let go.

For example, Robert had a fear of losing his wife Jan. To make sure she didn't leave, he hung on to her. His hanging on then pushed her further and further away. Robert was afraid of losing Jan because if she left him, this would reactivate[5] all his hurt of feeling not worth loving. To avoid this hurt. He hung on.

Once he was willing to feel his hurt, the loss of Jan ceased to be a treat. He no longer needed to hang on and became willing for her to leave. The moment this happened he changed the way he related to her. Instead of needing Jan, he started treasuring

么事，你要相信自己会没事，当你知道自己会走过去的时候，放手就相对容易了，相信也就是说出真相，无论发生什么事你真的不会有事。生活只有你在抵制拒绝它的时候才变得有威胁力。因此不要再抵制它了，相信无论发生什么事，你都会安然无恙。

放手的第二步是要愿意去感受你的伤痛。去体会所有的伤痛，去体会生活对你的愿望说不的那种感受。体会觉得自己一无是处或不够好的那种伤痛。

逃避伤痛就是使你抵制的原因，一旦你愿意去体会这种伤痛，你就不会抵制什么了，你就可以坦然地面对了。

举个例子吧，罗伯特害怕失去他的妻子简，为了确保她不离开自己，他把她守得牢牢的，看得紧紧的，结果却把她推得离自己越来越远了。罗伯特害怕失去简是因为如果她抛弃了他，他会觉得自己不值得爱了，这种伤痛会折磨他。为了避免这种伤害，他执拗地坚持着。

一旦他开始准备接受这种伤痛，就不会再有失去简的感觉了，他就不会再去苦苦纠缠而可以接受她的离去。一旦他能这么去想，他与她的关系就改变了。他开始信任她而不是需要她，简感受到罗伯特的浓情，也感受

④ **worthless**
/ˈwɜːθlɪs/
adj. 无用的

⑤ **reactivate**
/ˌriːˈæktɪveɪt/
v. 使恢复活力

her. Jan then felt so loved and able to be herself, she didn't want to leave.

This is what happens in life. The more you are able to let go and flow with life, the more life takes care of itself. You may not always get what you want, but you can always be free inside. You can restore both your peace of mind and your effectiveness. You can create a life that works.

到自己的人格受到了尊重，所以她就不会想要离开他了。

这就是生活，你越能坦然地面对一切，顺其自然，命运越能帮助走好人生。

你或许并不能总是如愿以偿，但你的内心却总能毫无羁绊，无拘无束，你既可以恢复内心的宁静，又可以恢复你生活的质量，你就可以创造一种幸福的生活了。

Eagles in a storm
暴风雨中的雄鹰

Remember, it is not the burdens of life that weigh us down, it is how we handle them.

切记，生活的重担本身并不能击垮我们，
关键是我们用怎样的心态去面对。

Did you know that an eagle[1] knows when a storm is approaching[2] long before it breaks?

The eagle will fly to some high spot and wait for the winds to come. When the storm hits, it sets its wings so that the wind will pick it up and lift it above the storm. While the storm rages below, the eagle is soaring[3] above it.

The eagle does not escape[4] the storm. It simply uses the storm to lift it higher. It rises on the winds that bring the storm.

When the storms of life come upon us — and all of us will experience them — we can rise above them by setting our minds and our belief toward God. The storms do not have to overcome us. We can allow God's power to lift us above them.

God enables us to ride the winds of the storm that bring sickness, tragedy[5], failure and disappointment in our lives. We can soar above the storm.

Remember, it is not the burdens[6] of life that weigh us down, it is how we handle them.

你知道么？老鹰能在暴风雨来临之前预知它将何时到来。

当暴风雨来临时，它会飞向高空，等待大风的来临。当暴风雨袭来时，它会张开双翅乘风飞得更高，凌于暴风雨之上，当猛烈的暴风雨来临时，它已在高空翱翔。

老鹰不会逃避暴风雨，而是在暴风雨中飞得更高，乘暴风雨前夕的风翱翔。

我们每个人都必须经历生活中的暴风雨，当他们袭来时，我们同样可以利用意志和虔诚的信念，凌于暴风雨之上。暴风雨并不能战胜我们，相反我们可以利用上帝的力量战胜他们。

上帝教会我们如何面对生活中的暴风雨（如疾病、悲剧、失败、失望等），我们同样可以翱翔于暴风雨中。

切记，生活的重担本身并不能击垮我们，关键是我们用怎样的心态去面对。

❶ eagle /ˈiːgl/
n. 鹰
❷ approach
/əˈprəʊtʃ/
v. 接近
❸ soar /sɔː/
vi. 升高，翱翔，高飞
❹ escape
/ɪˈskeɪp/
vi. 逃跑，逃脱
❺ tragedy
/ˈtrædʒədɪ/
n. 悲剧
❻ burden
/ˈbɜːdn/
n. 负担

Easy and difficult

难与易

Easy is to hurt someone who loves us
Difficult is to heal the wound

伤害爱我们的人容易
治愈他们的创伤难

Easy is to get a place in someone's address book
Difficult is to get a place in someone's heart

Easy is to judge the mistakes of others
Difficult is to recognize our own mistakes

Easy is to talk without thinking
Difficult is to refrain[1] the tongue

Easy is to hurt someone who loves us
Difficult is to heal the wound

Easy is to forgive others
Difficult is to ask for forgiveness

Easy is to set rules
Difficult is to follow them

Easy is to dream every night
Difficult is to fight for a dream

Easy is to show victory
Difficult is to assume defeat with dignity[2]

Easy is to admire a full moon
Difficult to see the other side

Easy is to stumble[3] with a stone

留在别人的地址薄里容易
留在别人的心中难

评价别人的错误容易
认识自己的错误难

信口开河容易
管住自己的嘴难

伤害爱我们的人容易
治愈他们的创伤难

原谅别人容易
让别人原谅难

制订规则容易
遵守规则难

每晚做梦容易
为梦想奋斗难

炫耀胜利容易
不失尊严地接受失败难

羡慕满月容易
看到月亮的背面难

被石头绊倒容易

❶ **refrain**
/rɪˈfreɪn/
v. 抑制

❷ **dignity**
/ˈdɪgnɪtɪ/
n. 高贵

❸ **stumble**
/ˈstʌmbl/
v. 绊倒

Difficult is to get up

Easy is to enjoy life every day
Difficult is to give it real value

Easy is to promise something to someone
Difficult is to fulfill[4] that promise

Easy is to say we love
Difficult is to show it every day

Easy is to criticize others
Difficult is to improve oneself

Easy is to make mistakes
Difficult is to learn from them

Easy is to weep[5] for a lost love
Difficult is to take care of it so as not to lose it

爬起来难

享受日常生活容易
追求生活真正价值的难

做出允诺容易
遵守允诺难

口头说爱容易
天天表现爱难

批评别人容易
提高自我难

犯错误容易
得到教训难

为失去之爱哭泣容易
珍惜爱不让之失去难

4 **fulfill**
/fʊlˈfɪl/
v. 实现
5 **weep**
/wiːp/
v. 哭泣

High and Lifted Up

飞呀，飞

Perhaps one day he would see what the old leaf had seen — perhaps.

或许有一天，他也将能够看到老树叶看到的——或许有那么一天。

It was a windy day.

The mailman barely[1] made it to the front door. When the door opened, Mrs. Pennington said, "hello", but, before she had a real chance to say "thank you", the mail blew out of the mailman's hands, into the house and the front door slammed in his face. Mrs. Pennington ran to pick up the mail.

"Oh my," she said.

Tommy was watching the shutters[2] open and then shut, open and then shut.

"Mom," he said, "may I go outside?"

"Be careful," she said. "It's so windy today."

Tommy crawled down from the window-seat and ran to the door. He opened it with a bang. The wind blew fiercely and snatched[3] the newly recovered mail from Mrs. Pennington's hands and blew it even further into the house.

"Oh my," she said again. Tommy ran outside and the door slammed shut.

Outside, yellow, gold, and red leaves were leaping from swaying trees, landing on the roof, jumping off the roof, and then chasing one another down the street in tiny whirlwinds[4] of merriment.

Tommy watched in fascination.

"If I was a leaf, I would fly clear across the world," Tommy

那是个有风的一天。

邮递员几乎不用走就到了前门。门开了，彭宁顿太太向他打招呼："你好。"她还未来得及说谢谢，邮递员手里拿着的邮件就被风刮进了房子。前门砰地被风关上了，彭宁顿太太跑过去捡起邮件。

"天哪！"彭宁顿太太感叹道。

汤姆看到窗户被风刮开，又关上；刮开又关上。

他说："妈妈我可以出去玩吗？"

"小心点儿，孩子。"她说："今天风很大"

汤姆从窗台上爬下来跑到门口。他呼地推开门，风很大，把彭宁顿太太刚刚捡起的邮件又刮进房子最里边了。

"天哪！"她又感叹道。汤姆跑出去了，门也关上了。

屋外黄色的、金色的、红色的树叶从摇曳的树上飘落下来，在风中飞舞。落到房顶上，又跳下来，然后欢天喜地地在街上你追我赶。

汤姆越看越着迷。

"如果我是一片树叶，我也可以飞遍全世界。"汤姆这样想着跑到院子里盘旋飞扬的五颜六色的树叶中间。

❶ barely
/ˈbeəlɪ/
adv. 几乎不能
❷ shutter
/ˈʃʌtə/
n. 百叶窗
❸ snatch
/snætʃ/
v. 拿取，攫取
❹ whirlwind
/ˈwɜːlwɪnd/
n. 旋风

thought and then ran out into the yard among the swirl of colors.

Mrs. Pennington came to the front porch. "Tommy, I have your jacket. Please put it on."

However, there was no Tommy in the front yard.

"Tommy? "

Tommy was a leaf. He was blowing down the street with the rest of his play-mates.

A maple leaf came close-by, touched him and moved ahead. Tommy met him shortly, brushed against him, and moved further ahead. They swirled around and around, hit cars and poles, flew up into the air and then down again.

"This is fun," Tommy thought.

The maple leaf blew in front of him. It was bright red with well-defined veins[5]. The sun-light shone through it giving it a brilliance never before seen by a little boy's eyes.

"Where do you think we are going? " Tommy asked the leaf.

"Does it matter? " the leaf replied. "Have fun. Life is short."

"I beg to differ," an older leaf said suddenly coming beside them. "The journey may be short, but the end is the beginning."

Tommy pondered this the best a leaf could ponder.

"Where do we end up? "

彭宁顿太太来到门廊说："汤姆，夹克，穿上你的夹克。"

汤姆已经跑得不见人影了。

"汤姆？"

汤姆像一片树叶一样和伙伴们在街上飞来飞去。

一片枫叶从汤姆面前飞过，碰了他一下，继续向前飞。汤姆对它一点儿也不客气，蹭了它一下，继续走自己的路。枫叶在风中盘旋地飞呀飞，撞到汽车上、电线杆上，飞向高空又落下来。

汤姆想："太好玩了"

一片枫叶飞到汤姆面前，那是一片纹理清晰的亮红色的枫叶。在阳光的照耀下显得更漂亮了。汤姆从来没见过这么漂亮的枫叶。

"你觉得我们会飞到哪儿？"汤姆问枫叶。

"那很重要吗？"枫叶答道："享受生活吧，生命是短暂的。"

"我可不想那样，"一片老树叶忽然出现在他们身边，说道："人生旅途短暂，终点便是起点。"

汤姆琢磨着老树叶说的这番话。

"那么何处是终点？"

"如果风把你吹向那个方向，"老树叶

❺ vein

/veɪn/

n. 叶脉，纹理

"If the wind blows you in that direction," the old leaf said, "you will end up in the city dump."

"I don't want that," Tommy said.

"If you are blown in that direction, you will fly high into the air and see things that no leaf has seen before."

"Follow me to the city dump," the maple leaf said. "Most of my friends are there."

The wind blew Tommy and the maple leaf along. Tommy thought of his choices. He wanted to continue to play.

"Okay," Tommy said, "I will go with you to the dump."

The winds shifted and Tommy and the leaf were blown in the direction of the city dump.

The old leaf didn't follow. He was blown further down the block and suddenly lifted up high into the air.

"Hey," he called out, "the sights up here. They are spectacular. Come and see."

Tommy and the maple leaf ignored[6] him.

"I see something. I see the dump." The old leaf cried out. "I see smoke. Come up here. I see fire."

"I see nothing," the maple leaf said.

Tommy saw the fence that surrounded the city dump. He was happy to be with his friend. They would have fun in the dump.

说："城市垃圾场便是终点站。"

汤姆说："我可不想去那鬼地方。"

"如果你被风吹到那个方向，你就会飞向高空，看到别人看不到的东西。"

"跟我去城市垃圾场，"枫叶说："我的很多朋友都在那里。"

风吹着汤姆和枫叶向前走，汤姆不知自己该做何选择.但他想接着玩。

"好吧！"汤姆答应道："我跟你去垃圾场。"

风向变了，汤姆和枫叶顺风被吹向垃圾场。

老树叶却不跟随他们。他逆着风向飞，突然被风吹到了高空。

他大声叫道："嗨！看这儿的风景，多美多壮观，快来看呀！"

汤姆和枫叶不理睬他。

"我看到了好多东西，看到了垃圾场，"老树叶叫喊道："我看到了烟，到这儿来，我看到了火。"

枫叶说："我什么也看不到。"

汤姆看见围绕着垃圾场的围墙。他很希望能和朋友们在一起，朋友们在垃圾场一定玩得很愉快。

突然，一辆小轿车停在垃圾场附近，是

Suddenly, a car pulled up. It was Tommy's mom. Mrs. Pennington wasn't about to let her little boy run into the city dump.

"Not so fast," she said getting out of the car. "You are not allowed to play in there. Don't you see the smoke? "

Tommy watched the maple leaf blow against the wall and struggle to get over. He ran over to get it but was unable to reach it.

Mrs. Pennington walked over and took the leaf. She put it in her pocket.

"There," she said, "it will be safe until we get home."

Tommy smiled, ran to the car and got in. He rolled down the back window and looked up into the sky. He wondered where the old leaf had gone. Perhaps one day he would see what the old leaf had seen — perhaps.

汤姆的母亲，她不想让汤姆去垃圾场。

"别跑那么快，"她边下车边喊道："不许你到那儿玩，没看到那儿冒烟吗？"

汤姆看到枫叶撞到墙上，又努力站稳，他跑过去想拉住枫叶，但是够不着。

彭宁顿太太走过去，抓住枫叶，把它放在口袋里。

"待在这里面"她说"回到家就安全了。"

汤姆笑了，跑向车子，上车后，把后车窗摇下来，看着外边的天空，他想知道老树叶飞到哪儿去了。或许有一天，他也将能够看到老树叶看到的——或许有那么一天。

❻ ignore

/ɪɡˈnɔː/

v. 不理睬，忽视

Homework

家庭作业

Jason always hated downloading his homework into his brain. He swore it was the longest two minutes of the day.

贾森不愿意把作业下载到自己的大脑里，他发誓这是他一天中感到最长的两分钟。

"Have you done your homework? "

"Oh mom! "

"Quit playing with the dog and get in that bedroom and do your homework! "

Jason reluctantly[1] released the sock that he had been pulling from Cocoa's mouth and the dog stood there in silence, waiting for her master to return to playing their game of tug-of-war.

"Can't a kid have some fun? "

"You've had enough fun today. Right now, it's time for your homework."

"Listen to your mother," the father insisted. "I told you how important your homework is."

"Oh yeah, like my whole life's gonna end if I don't do my stupid homework."

"Hey, young man, you watch your mouth! " The father had been reading the evening paper from the family room couch but now he directed his full attention to his sarcastic[2] son. Jason remained on the floor near Cocoa, fully expecting a tongue-lashing by his father. He was determined to remain defiant[3], but his father's large imposing stature and the swiftness with which he was

"做完作业了吗?"

"知道了,妈妈。"

"别跟狗玩了,回卧室做作业。"

贾森很不情愿放下从小狗可可嘴里夺回的袜子。可可一声不响地站在那里等着主人再和它玩一次玩拔河游戏.

"难道小孩子就不能玩玩吗? "

"今天你玩得时间够长啦!现在该做作业了。"

"听妈妈的话,"爸爸坚持道:"我不是给你讲过作业的重要性了吗? "

"知道了,……好像如果我不做那无聊的作业世界末日就要到了。"

"嗨小家伙! 你怎么能这样说话?"方才还坐在客厅沙发上看晚报的父亲,现在却把注意转移到话中带刺的儿子身上。贾森仍坐在地上守着小狗,猜想父亲一定会给他一巴掌。他打算反抗到底,但父亲那高大的身材及抽出皮带打他的架势打消了他这个念头。

"今年我们对你管教不严,你的学习成绩直线下降,这种情况也该改变了。从现在起,晚饭后你要自觉完成家庭作业,不要再让家人提醒了。"

贾森用拳头敲了一下软绵绵地铺着地毯

❶ reluctantly
/rɪˈlʌktəntlɪ/
adv. 不情愿地
❷ sarcastic
/sɑːˈkæstɪk/
adj. 讽刺的
❸ defiant
/dɪˈfaɪənt/
adj. 挑衅的

capable of pulling out his belt, quickly diminished his boldness.

"We've been too lenient on you this year and your grades are down. But that's gonna change. From now on I want you to automatically do that homework of yours after dinner. And I don't want to have to tell you about it, again."

Jason slammed his fist into the soft, carpeted floor before rising. He was aware of his disobedience[4], yet he wished to make a stand. "I don't know what the big deal is," he sharply replied.

"The big deal is: we want you to have a future."

"I don't understand what's wrong with you kids today," the mother chided him. "They can't make it any easier for you."

"Oh right, like it was so much harder when YOU were kids." Jason's insolent[5] response surprised even him.

"You're damn right it was," the father argued. He hopped off the couch and approached his defiant son. "We didn't have all the luxuries like you kids have today. And we didn't talk back to our parents the way you kids do."

"It's tougher being a kid today," Jason declared, slowly backing away from his father. "You didn't have all the problems we have. We have a lot more pressure today."

的地板，才站了起来，他意识到自己在默默地反抗了，他仍想坚持自己的立场，不服气地答道："我觉得没什么大不了的。"

"问题是我们希望你能有前途."

"我搞不明白你们现在的孩子都怎么了，"妈妈责怪道："这么让人费心。"

"是的，但你们小时候更让人费心。"贾森的强词夺理，连他自己都感到惊奇。

"你简直是个常有理，"父亲争论道。他从长沙发上跳下来，走到倔强的儿子跟前说："我们小时候没有你们现在这么多奢侈品，也没有像你一样，竟敢这样跟长辈顶嘴。"

"今天的孩子们更难。"贾森辩驳道，边说边往后退。"你们那时不需要面对我们今天这么多问题，我们承受着更多的压力。"

"就算你说得有道理，你总是有理。回你房间做作业，待在那儿一晚上都不要出来."

"我做错什么了？"贾森惊讶地问道。

"你心里清楚你做错了什么，你最好闭上你的嘴，我受够你苛薄的话了。"

贾森跑出客厅，顺着大厅穿堂走到自己的卧室，可可摇着尾巴，老老实实地跟着他。

❹ disobedience
/ˌdɪsəˈbiːdjəns/
n. 不服从，违抗

❺ insolent
/ˈɪnsələnt/
adj. 无礼的

"All right, just for that, you're grounded! Now get in that room of yours and do your homework! And stay there for the rest of the night."

"What did I do?" Jason cried out in surprise.

"You know very well what you did! You better start watching that mouth of yours, boy, 'cause I've about had it with your sarcastic remarks!"

Jason stormed out of the family room and headed down the hallway to his bedroom. Cocoa loyally followed him, wagging her tail.

The mother and father gazed at each other in silence for several lingering[6] moments. Their son's laziness was becoming a growing problem and they were uncertain how to handle it. His behavior baffled them because they had always stressed the importance of work to their son. Where had he developed such apathy? They shook their heads in dismay before resuming their prior activities.

The father returned his attention to the evening paper which was displayed on the family room ceiling-viewer. He floated comfortably two feet above the flat, bed-shaped, anti-gravity couch, with his arms folded casually behind his head. "Turn to Sports," he commanded. Page one of the Sports' section instantly appeared on the ceiling-viewer.

父亲和母亲对视无语，儿子的懒惰越来越成为一个令人担忧的问题。他们甚至不知道该怎么办才好。儿子的言行举止也让他们困惑。尽管他们一再强调作业的重要性，但儿子对此漠不关心。他们失望地摇摇头，然后各干各的。

父亲接着读显示在天花板上的晚报，两脚搭在平坦的床式悬空长沙发上，两手抱臂随意放在脑后，他命令道："转到体育新闻。"体育版面的第一页出现在天花板的浏览器上。

母亲斜卧在变形摇椅上，摇椅能自动地调节形状，以提供最大的舒适度，她伸手拿起可以控制整个房间的电脑控制板，按了一下红键之后命令道："奥赛罗"。色彩鲜明，栩栩如生的由电脑生成的演员全息图出现在客厅里，莎士比亚的古典戏剧开始上演了。她的左手紧紧握着驱压球以驱除身心的紧张和焦虑。

"我想我们不要把孩子逼得太紧，"母亲不安地提醒孩子的父亲："你知道，逼急了对孩子没什么好处。"

"小孩子从小就该懂得生活的艰难。"父亲坚持地答道："没有人可以帮助你，必须靠自己奋斗。"边说边伸手去拿放在托盘上的

❻ lingering
/ˈlɪŋgərɪŋ/
adj. 逗留不去的，延迟的

The mother reclined on the shape-shifting rocking chair, which naturally altered its shape to provide the maximum comfort to its host. She reached over to the house's computer control panel, pressed a red button and ordered, "Othello, please." Colorful, life-like, computer generated, hologram[7] actors suddenly appeared in their family room and began to act out Shakespeare's classical play. Her left hand tightly gripped her Tension-Ball, which absorbed all the stress and anxiety from her mind and body.

"I hope we aren't pushing him too much," the mother noted worriedly. "You know, it's not good to push a child too much, either."

The boy's got to learn that life's not easy," the father firmly replied. "No one's gonna hand you anything today. You have to work for it." He reached out and grabbed a snack made, and served to him on a tray, by their government-issued robot.

"Ray, please," he commanded, as he munched on his delectable after-dinner snack. An invisible beam was instantly emitted from the anti-gravity couch and was directed at its occupant. Gentle bursts of stress-relieving heat and comforting waves of inaudible sound, vibrated and massaged his aching back and his stiff neck. "These four-hour work days are killing me," he mumbled to himself.

"I hope we're doing the right thing."

小吃，小吃是被控制的机器人端上来的。

"请放射。"他边嚼着美味的小吃边命令道．一道肉眼看不到的光线刹那间从悬空的长沙发里放射出来，射到贾森父亲身上。一种能减轻压力的热能温和地放射出来，一种低微的令人舒适的声波传送过来，震动着，按摩着他疼痛的背部和僵硬的颈部。"每天4小时工作简直要我的命。"他自言自语道。

"我希望我们做的是对的。"

"孩子觉得一切都是理所当然的。"父亲生气地打断母亲的话："我们不能让孩子再这样下去。"

"我想也是，"母亲轻声地答道。她闭着双眼，先前的争论引起的忧虑已使她身心俱疲，她开始进入沉沉的舒适的睡眠中。

待在自己卧室的贾森生气极了，他气愤地用力把枕头摔到墙上。然后极不情愿地做起作业来了。

"他们根本不懂。"他痛苦地抱怨道，他在说给小狗可可听："现在的情况要比他们当年复杂得多，他们压根儿就不懂现在的孩子是什么样子。"

但既然对于他的问题不存在别的合理的解决办法，他只能先把不满和牢骚放在一边了。他把作业磁盘插入电脑，握着长长的接

7 hologram
/ˈhɒləʊɡræm/
n. 全息图

"That boy's taking everything for granted," the father abruptly added in anger. "And we've got to put a stop to it right now."

"I guess so," the mother softly replied. Her eyes were already closed — her mind and body drained of all the anxiety that was the result of the previous argument. She was beginning to drift into a deep, relaxing sleep.

Jason was fuming in his bedroom. He hurled his pillow against the wall in indignation before brusquely[8] grabbing his homework assignment for the night.

"They don't understand," he bitterly complained, directing his comments to Cocoa. "Things are tougher today. They don't have any idea what it's like being a kid."

But since no reasonable alternative to his problem existed, he reluctantly placed aside his resentment and began to work. He inserted the homework disk into his player, grabbed the long connecting cord, and inserted its metal end into the socket in the back of his head. Like everyone else, his cerebral socket had been implanted[9] at birth.

Jason always hated downloading his homework into his brain. He swore it was the longest two minutes of the day.

线绳，然后把接线绳金属端插入自己大脑后部的插孔中。像其他人一样，贾森大脑上的插孔是在他出生时就植入到大脑里的。

　　贾森不愿意把作业下载到自己的大脑里，他发誓这是他一天中感到最长的两分钟。

❽ brusquely
/ˈbrʊsklɪ/
adv. 粗鲁地
❾ implant
/ɪmˈplɑːnt/

A touching story

感人的故事

Inside was a drawing in bright crayon of a yellow beach, a blue sea, and a brown bird. Underneath was carefully printed: A SANDPIPER TO BRING YOU JOY.

信封里面是一幅用蜡笔画的画：黄色的沙滩，蓝蓝的海洋，一只棕色的鸟。画的下方写道：带给你快乐的矶鹞。

She was six years old when I first met her on the beach near where I live. She was building a sandcastle or something and looked up, her eyes as blue as the sea.

"Hello! " she said. I answered with a nod, not really in the mood to bother with a small child. "I'm building," she said. "I see that. What is it? " I asked, not caring. "Oh, I don't know, I just like the feel of the sand." That sounds good, I thought. A sand-piper[1] glided[2] by. "That's a joy," the child said. "It's what?" "It's a joy. My mama says sandpipers come to bring us joy." The bird glided down the beach. "Good-bye joy," I muttered to myself, "hello pain," and turned to walk on. I was depressed; my life seemed completely out of balance. "What's your name? " She wouldn't give up. "Robert," I answered. "I'm Robert Peterson. " "Mine's Wendy... I'm six." "Hi, Wendy." She giggled. "You're funny," she said. In spite of my gloom I laughed too and walked on. Her musical giggle followed me. "Come again, Mr. P," she called. "We'll have another happy day."

The days and weeks that followed belonged to others: PTA meetings, and an ailing[3] mother. The sun was shining one morning as I took my hands out of the dishwater. "I need a sand-piper," I said to myself. The breeze was chilly, but I strode along, trying to recapture[4] the serenity I needed. I had forgotten the child and was startled when she appeared.

"Hello, Mr. P," she said. "Do you want to play? " "What did you have in mind? " I asked, with a twinge[5] of annoyance. "I don't

第一次在沙滩遇到她时，她才只有6岁。那时，她正在用沙子堆建城堡或其它的东西，她抬起头来看看我，她的眼睛是那么的清澈。

"你好！"她说。我只是点了点头，因为我不想让一个小孩子左右我的思绪。"我正在搭东西，"她说道。"我看到了。你搭什么呢？"我不太关切地问道。"噢，我也不知道我搭的是什么，我只是喜欢沙子的感觉。"听起来不错，我暗想。这时一只矶鹬从我们身边飞过去。"那是一种幸福和愉悦，"孩子说道。"那是什么？""是幸福和愉悦。妈妈说矶鹬是给我们带来快乐的。"那只鸟飞落到沙滩上。"再见了我的幸福，"我继续沿着沙滩走着，轻声地对自己说，"我开始的将是痛苦和辛酸。"我是那么的沮丧，我的生活完全失去了重心。"你叫什么名字？"她追问到。"罗伯特，"我答道，"罗伯特·皮特森。""我叫温迪，我6岁了。""你好，温迪。"她格格地笑起来了。"你真有趣，"她说道。尽管我的心情很忧郁，我还是笑了，沿着沙滩继续走着。她那悦耳的笑声包围着我。"皮特森，你要再来呀，"她冲我喊道，"我们还会再有一个快乐的日子。"

接下来的日子都被PTA会议以及卧病在床的妈妈占据着。那天，天气是那么晴朗，

❶ sandpiper
/ˈsændpaɪpə/
n. 矶鹬

❷ glide
/glaɪd/
v. 滑行

❸ ailing
/ˈeɪlɪŋ/
adj. 生病的，有病的

❹ recapture
/ˌriːˈkæptʃə/
v. 再次体验，再次经历

❺ twinge
/twɪndʒ/
n. 一阵（不愉快的）思绪

know, you say." "How about charades？ " I asked sarcastically. The tinkling laughter burst forth again. "I don't know what that is." "Then lets just walk." Looking at her, I noticed the delicate fairness of her face. "Where do you live?" I asked. "Over there." She pointed toward a row of cottages. "Where do you go to school？ " "I don't go to school. Mommy says we're on vacation." She chattered little girl talk as we strolled up the beach, but my mind were on other things. When I left for home, Wendy said it had been a happy day. Feeling surprisingly better, I smiled at her and agreed.

Three weeks later, I rushed to my beach in a state of near panic. I was in no mood to even greet Wendy. "Look, if you don't mind," I said crossly when Wendy caught up with me, "I'd rather be alone today." She seemed unusually pale and out of breath. "Why？ " she asked. I turned to her and shouted, "Because my mother died！ " and thought, "My God, why was I saying this to a little child？ " "Oh," she said quietly, "then this is a bad day." "Yes," I said, "and yesterday, and the day before and oh just go away！ " "Did it hurt？ " she inquired. "Did what hurt？ " I was exasperated with her, with myself. I strode off.

A month or so after that, when I next went to the beach, she wasn't there. Feeling guilty, ashamed and admitting to myself I missed her, went up to the cottage after my walk and knocked on the door. A drawn looking woman opened the door.

"Hello," I said. "I'm Robert Peterson. I missed your little girl to-

我腾出了手里的活，"我要去沙滩听听矶鹞的声音，"我暗自想到。海风凉飕飕的，我沿着沙滩慢慢地走，重新体验着我需要的那份宁静。

"你好，彼特森，"那个小女孩突然出现在我面前，看到她我很吃惊，因为我几乎把她忘了。"你想和我一起玩吗？"她问。"你想玩什么呢？"我不快地回应道。"我不知道，你说。""玩字谜？"我带着讽刺的口吻说。银铃般地笑声又迸发出来。"那是什么，我不会玩。""那我们就走走吧。"我看了看她，发现她的表情是那么的明媚。"你住哪儿？"我问道。"就在那儿。"她指着那边的一排排小屋。"你在哪儿上学？""我不上学。妈妈说我们在度假。"她一直在喋喋不休地说着，而我却在想着别的事。我要回家了，温迪说今天她非常高兴。突然间，我觉得我的心情好了很多，我微笑地看着她，告诉她我也很高兴。

三周后，我几乎疯狂地再次跑到海滩来，我没有心情向温迪打招呼。当她紧跟着我想和我说话时，我很不高兴地说道："如果你不介意的话，我今天想一个人待着。"她的脸色异常的苍白，她几乎喘不过气来，"为什么？"她问道。我冲她大叫道："我妈妈去世

day and wondered where she was? " "Oh yes, Mr. Peterson, please come in. Wendy spoke of you so much. I'm afraid I allowed her to bother you. If she was a nuisance, please accept my apologies." "Not at all — she's a delightful child, " I said. "Wendy died last week, Mr. Peterson. She had leukemia[6]. Maybe she didn't tell you." Struck dumb, I groped for a chair. I had to catch my breath. "She loved this beach; so when she asked to come, we couldn't say no. She seemed so much better here and had a lot of what she called happy days. But the last few weeks, she declined rapidly..." Her voice faltered[7], "She left something for you...if only I can find it. Could you wait a moment while I look? " I nodded stupidly, my mind racing for something, to say to this lovely young woman. She handed me a smeared[8] envelope, with MR. P printed in bold childish letters. Inside was a drawing in bright crayon of a yellow beach, a blue sea, and a brown bird. Underneath was carefully printed: A SANDPIPER TO BRING YOU JOY.

Tears welled up in my eyes. I took Wendy's mother in my arms. "I'm so sorry, I'm so sorry. I'm so sorry," I muttered over and over, and we wept together.

The precious little picture is framed now and hangs in my study. Six words one for each year of her life — that speak to me of harmony, courage, and undemanding love. A gift from a child with sea-blue eyes and hair the color of sand — who taught me the gift of love. Life is so complicated, the hustle[9] and bustle[10] of everyday traumas[11] can make us lose focus about what is truly

了!"我暗想道,"天哪,我为什么要和一个小女孩说这些话呢?""噢,"她安静地说,"那真是太不幸了。""是的,"我说道,"昨天,前天,都那么的难过,让所有的一切都过去吧!""你感觉很受伤吗?"她询问道。"什么受伤?"我对她、对自己感到很是恼怒,于是我离开了海滩。

大约一个月后,我再次来到那儿,但是却没发现她。我感到抱歉、内疚,我承认我有点儿想念她。散步后,我走到小屋前,我敲了敲门。一个面色疲惫的妇女开了门。

"你好,"我说道。"我是罗伯特·皮特森。我很想念你的小女孩,她在哪儿呢?""噢,皮特森先生,请进。温迪经常提到你。很抱歉她打扰您了,如果她真的招人烦,请接受我的抱歉。""不烦,她很有趣,经常逗我开怀大笑。"我答道。"皮特森先生,上周温迪已经去世了,她得了白血病,她可能没告诉你。"我目瞪口呆地愣在了那儿,我赶忙扶住了椅子,几乎窒息。"她喜欢那个海滩,所以只要她想去那儿,我们从不阻拦。她的状况好了很多,自从她去了海滩后,她称那些日子非常美妙。但是,前几周她的状况急剧下降。"她的声音变得软弱无力。"她送了一些东西给你,如果我能找到的话。我去找

⑥ **leukemia**
/ljuːˈkiːmɪə/
n. 白血病

⑦ **falter**
/ˈfɔːltə/
v. 慢慢而行

⑧ **smear**
/smɪə/
v. 抹擦使变模糊

⑨ **hustle**
/ˈhʌsl/
n. 奔忙

⑩ **bustle**
/ˈbʌsl/
n. 匆匆忙忙

⑪ **trauma**
/ˈtrɔːmə/
n. 损伤

important. This week, be sure to give your loved ones an extra hug; and by all means, take a moment, even if it is only ten seconds, to stop and smell the roses.

找看，你能等一会儿吗？"我木讷地点了点头，想找些话对这可亲的年轻妇人说。她递给我一个有些模糊的信封，上面写着皮特森先生，字迹是那么的孩子气。信封里面是一幅用蜡笔画的画：黄色的沙滩，蓝蓝的海洋，一只棕色的鸟。画的下方写道：带给你快乐的矶鹞。

泪水在眼里打转，我拥抱了温迪的妈妈。"对不起，对不起，对不起，"我喃喃自语地说着，然后，我们一起痛哭了起来。

这幅非常珍贵的图片被我镶了边，挂在书房里。画面上每个字代表了她生命中的每一年，对我来说，这些字的内涵就是：和谐、勇气和毫不吝啬的爱。这个有着海洋般蔚蓝色的眼睛、沙滩般金黄头发的小姑娘，送给我这么一份珍贵礼物，她教会了我爱的真谛。生活是复杂的，整日的奔忙以及心灵上的创伤使我们意识不到那些对我们真正重要的东西。这周，不要忘记给你所爱的人一个拥抱，并且抽出时间，哪怕只有10秒钟去闻闻花香。

Last you a life time

约你一生

If you go out with me this time, I promise it will last a life time.

如果你这次跟我一块出去的话，我保证，这次约会的时间会很长很长，像一辈子那样长。

Young Ashley was having a great end of the summer party at her house. She invited all of her friends to come over and go swimming in her lake. One of her best friends Zech was there. Not only was he one of her best friends, but also her ex-boyfriend, but it didn't bother her too much.

Well, as everyone was jumping off the <u>diving board</u>[1] and swimming in the lake Ashley walked up stairs to go get her sunglasses. Zack slowly followed her up stairs.

Ashley grabbed[2] the sunglasses . "Get off! " she yelled[3] as she walked out of her room back down stairs. Again Zech slowly followed.

"What are you doing? " asked Ashley. Zech was following her like a lost puppy dog. Ashley went back outside and jumped in holding on to her sun glasses, then she stuck them back on as she climbing into a raft[4] and laid there trying to get a tan.

"Hey, any of you kids want some more drinks? We're running low." said Ashley's mom. "Yeah. Grab us some more cherry coke please," yelled Ashley from in the water and then her mom drove off in her car.

"Hey, your mom is gone. Can we go to your room? " asked Zech. "NO! " said Ashley, talking to another friend of hers, Jordan.

暑期末，阿什利在家里举办了一次假期聚会。她邀请了许多好朋友，并与他们在自己的游泳池里游泳。她最好的朋友泽卡也在那儿。泽卡不仅是她最好的朋友之一，同时也是她的前任男朋友，但是这并没有给她带来不便。当每个人从跳板上跳入水中，并在游泳池里畅游时，阿什利上楼去取太阳镜。泽卡这时也跟着她上了楼。

阿什利拿到眼镜，走出房间下楼了，这时她大喊着说："走开。"泽卡还是跟着她。

阿什利追问道："你想做什么？"泽卡有如一条迷失的小狗跟着她。

阿什利从屋子里走出来后，拿着太阳镜，跳入水中，然后她爬上一个充气筏，戴上眼镜，躺在上面晒太阳。

阿什利的妈妈问道："孩子们要再来些饮料吗？我们快要走了。"阿什利在水中喊道："再给我们拿些樱桃可乐吧。"然后，她妈妈开车就走了。

泽卡说道："嘿，你妈妈走了，去你房间行吗？"阿什利正在和乔丹讲话，她立刻答道："不行。"

乔丹说："阿什利，泽卡喜欢你。"阿什利说："才不是呢，他只是想要更多的东西。"乔丹说："不对，他只是不知道怎样约你出

❶ diving board
跳板
❷ grab
/græb/
v. 攫取，夺取
❸ yell
/jel/
v. 大声叫
❹ raft
/rɑːft/
n. 充气救生筏

"Ashley, he likes you." said Jordan. "No, he just wants some," said Ashley. "No he just doesn't know how to ask you out," said Jordan. "He already did that twice, the 1st time lasted 3 days and the 2nd time lasted 12 hrs," said Ashley. "That's why he is afraid to ask you out, because you might say no," said Jordan.

"Well, if he ask, I would," said Ashley as she jumped into the lake and splashed[5] Raven and Katie. "Ashley!" yelled Katie. Raven laughed because Katie looked liked a drowned[6] rat. "You look funny," said Raven.

"Ashley, I see Zech, can I tell him what you said? " asked Jordan. "Whatever," said Ashley as she swam under the dock.

"Hey, Jordan, can I talk to you? " asked Zech. "Yeah, sure." Zack and Jordan walked the porch in the front and sat down.

"Jordan , will Ashley go out with me if I ask her? " asked Zech. "Yeah, she said she would," said Jordan. "Ok. Well, I need to get her alone," said Zack. " I help your guys alone," said Jordan. "Thanks man," said Zech. "No problem," said Jordan.

"Ashley, someone wants to talk to you." Ashley got out and wrapped a towel around herself. "Yes? " then she saw Zech. She sat down next to him. "Ashley, I know every time we go out it last shorter and shorter, but if you go out with me this time, I promise

去。"阿什利说:"他已经约我两次了,第一次花了3天,第二次花了12个小时。"乔丹说:"那就是为什么他害怕约你出去,因为他怕你拒绝。"

阿什利说道:"好吧,如果这次他约我,我会答应的。"而后,阿什利又跳入水池中,把拉文和卡蒂都溅湿了。卡蒂大喊道:"阿什利!"拉文笑着说:"你太好笑了。"因为卡蒂此时就像落汤鸡一样。

乔丹说:"阿什利,我去找泽卡,我能把你说的话告诉他吗?"阿什利游到池边答道:"可以。"

泽卡问道:"嘿,乔丹我能跟你谈谈吗?"乔丹答道:"当然可以。"两人走到前面的走廊处,坐下来交谈。

泽卡问道:"乔丹,如果我约阿什利,她愿意跟我出去吗?"乔丹答道:"当然,她说过她愿意。"

泽卡说道:"太好了,我要单独跟她谈谈。"

乔丹说道:"我帮你,让你们俩单独在一起。"泽卡说道:"谢谢你了。"乔丹说道:"别客气。"

"阿什利,有人想跟你谈谈。"阿什利走出来,身上裹了一块浴巾,"什么?"她看了

⑤ splash
/splæʃ/
v. 飞溅,溅湿
⑥ drown
/draʊn/
v. 淹死,溺死

it will last a life time." Ashley was so touched by what he said she gave him a huge kiss.

"I guess that is a Yes？" asked Zac, shocked about her kiss. "Yes！" said Ashley with tears in her eyes.

看泽卡，然后挨着他坐下来。"阿什利，我知道每次和你出去玩儿的时间越来越短，但是如果你这次跟我一块出去的话，我保证，这次约会的时间会很长很长，像一辈子那样长。"

阿什利非常感动，她给了泽卡一个深深的吻，泽卡问道："我猜想你同意了？"阿什利满含泪水的说道："当然啦！"

Caught by her smile
令人心醉的微笑

I waited for around 5mins then, she appeared. She was wearing that same smile that caught me.

我等了她5分钟之后,她出现了,脸上依旧挂着那甜美的微笑, 那微笑是那么的迷人。

Well like most authors I am one who do not believe in love at first sight untill I experienced it myself.

It all started like this, I was with a few friends at McDonalds, after my lecture from school, we were chatting and laughing at some stupid stories that one of my friends told.

Just then, a group of girls came and took their seats, there was this girl, quite outstanding[1] for that striking[2] red top she was wearing and she had this sweet smile.

Then, while they were at the counter, ordering their food, I noticed something, they all had a disability, and they could not talk. But, this was not considered a disability to me, I walked up to them, and ask for her number, well, she was surprised.

But, she eventually[3] gave me her address and her name is Elaine, she did not have a phone at home and there was no possibility to talk to her.

After a few days, I sent her a letter, asking her out on a date the following Saturday. Whether she agreed to the date or was it rejected[4], I could not tell for I did not know!

We were supposed to meet at the Lido cinema to catch a movie; I waited for around 5mins then, she appeared. She was wearing that same smile that caught me.

像所有的作家一样，我不相信一见钟情，直到那次我亲身体验了这种感觉。

故事是这样发生的，从学校讲课回来，我和一些朋友到了麦当劳，我们讨论着一位朋友给我们讲述的可笑的故事，我们边聊边开怀大笑。

就在那时，进来一群女孩，她们找了位子坐下来，其中一个女孩是那么显眼，与众不同，她穿了一件红上衣，脸上挂着甜美的微笑。

然后，当她们来到柜台前点食物时，我才注意到她们都不能讲话，但是，对我来说，这并不算是残疾。我走近她们，问她的电话号码，她很是惊奇。

但是，她最后还是给了我她的住址和姓名，她叫伊莱恩，她家没有电话，因为她不能讲话……

过了几天，我给她寄了一封信，约她下周六出来约会。她能否接受我的邀请，我也不知道。

我们约在利多影院见面，一起看电影。我等了她5分钟之后，她出现了，脸上依旧挂着那甜美的微笑，那微笑是那么的迷人。

我们看的影片名叫《冰河世纪》，为了顺利交流，我需要纸和笔。

❶ outstanding
/aʊtˈstændɪŋ/
adj. 显著的，杰出的

❷ striking
/ˈstraɪkɪŋ/
adj. 显著的

❸ eventually
/ɪˈventjʊəlɪ/
adv. 最后地

❹ reject
/rɪˈdʒekt/
v. 拒绝

In the cinema, we saw he show "Ice Age." In order to communicate[5], I needed to get a pen and paper.

I asked her about how she felt about me. She told me she was very happy, but at the same time, she was worried as she could not define[6] whether my love was out of sympathy or was it from my heart.

From that moment, I have been asking myself the question, until a month later after my exams, I finally made up my mind, I was really in love with her, not for her disability that I sympathize[7], not for that she is pretty, but for the fact that I love her... I went to her home, which made her quite surprised, I pulled her out of her home and ran to the park in font of her block of flats. I looked at her and wrote to her how I felt, she looked at me with those big black eyes, those that could take your soul away if you were staring at them for a long time.

She took the pen and wrote this sentence, "I love you too, but now that I am assured that you love me for what I am and not out of sympathy, I feel that I will not regret the decision."

Now, we have been together for two years and although we have not planned to get married, I have never once quarrel with her, not even on paper and I never will...

　　我问她对我感觉如何，她说她非常高兴，但是她不敢肯定我对她的爱是出于同情还是发自内心。

　　从那时起，我不停地问自己这个同样的问题。考试结束后，我终于下定了决心，我意识到我真的爱她，我对她的爱不是出于同情，也不是因为她的美貌，而是因为我真的爱她。我去了她家，这使她很诧异。我把她从家里拽出来，来到了她家街区前的一个公园里。我看着她，把我对她的爱意都写在了纸上，她用那大大的黑眼睛看着我，那大大的眼睛简直是勾人魂魄，如果盯着她多看一会儿的话，真有灵魂出壳的感觉。

　　她拿起笔，这样写道，"我也爱你，我现在知道，你不是出于同情而爱我，而是真的喜欢我本人，我不会后悔和你在一起的选择。"

　　现在，我们在一起已经两年了，尽管我们还没有结婚的打算，但是，我从来没和她吵过架，从来没用纸和笔和她吵过架，而且，我永远也不会和她吵架……

⑤ communicate
/kəˈmjuːnɪkeɪt/
v. 交流

⑥ define
/dɪˈfaɪn/
v. 解释

⑦ sympathize
/ˈsɪmpəθaɪz/
v. 同情

By chance and by choices
前生注定的缘分

We shivered with a delicious horror at the opportunity, the life — our lives — that would have been missed.

我们对这样千载难逢的机会感到既甜蜜又害怕得浑身颤抖，生命——我们的生命——一不留神，就会擦肩而过。

My father met my mother in a poker game. He said she was the best bluffer[1] he'd ever seen. She sat with five men at a table under an elm[2] tree that shaded them from the hot Kansas City, Missouri. Her talent for subterfuge[3] lay hidden behind her sweet, serene[4] smile. She beat them all. My father couldn't take his eyes off her.

It was her company's annual picnic, and he walked her home. The next week, from his home in Chicago, he sent her a post card: "Remember me? Please do, 'cause I'll be calling you one of these days. David."

She still has that. I'm not sure what made her save it. Though he already had his heart set on her, she hadn't chosen him yet, at least not consciously.

As my father often told us while we were growing up, it was blind luck that he was at the picnic that day. A salesman for a big electronics company, he was in town to meet with clients and happened to stop by the branch office that Saturday morning to make some calls. The telephone rang: it was the manager of a local radio station with whom my father had done some business. "Dave! Glad you're in town! " he said, and invited him to come right over to their annual picnic.

My mother was a writer at that radio station. If my father hadn't stopped by the office that morning, he told us, or if he'd

我的父亲和母亲是在一次打牌时邂逅的。父亲说母亲是他有生以来见到的出牌高手。赤日炎炎，她跟五个男人坐在密苏里州堪萨斯城榆荫下的一张桌边。她脸上挂着甜甜的、圣洁的微笑，却出手老练、隐而不露，将他们统统打败。我的父亲怎么也无法将目光从她的身上移开。

这是一年一度的野餐聚会。随后，父亲送她回家。又过了一个星期，父亲从芝加哥的家里给她寄去了一张明信片，上面写道："还记得我吗？请记住吧，因为这些天我会给你打电话的。戴维。"

如今，她仍保留着那张明信片。我拿不准究竟是什么让她保留了下来。尽管他已经一门心思都放在了她的身上，但她还没有决定选择他，至少潜意识中还没有这样。

在我们作子女的逐渐成长的岁月中，父亲经常告诉我们说那天野餐会他是无意中撞了一个好运。作为一家大型电子公司的推销员，他进城是要会见客户，那个星期六上午碰巧停在分公司，准备打几个电话。这时，电话铃响了起来：正好是当地广播电台的经理，我的父亲要和他做一笔生意。"戴维！很高兴你进城来！"那位经理说，然后邀请父亲过去参加他们的年度野餐会。

❶ bluffer
/ˈblʌfə/
n. 吓唬人的人

❷ elm
/elm/
n. 榆树

❸ subterfuge
/ˈsʌbtəfjuːdʒ/
n. 诡计；手段

❹ serene
/sɪˈriːn/
adj. 平静的；宁静的

gotten there two minutes later... we shivered[5] with a delicious horror at the opportunity, the life-our lives — that would have been
missed.

My mother saw him when he was in town, but she dated
other men, including a car salesman who entered our family lore.
Soon after she met my father, the car salesman gave her a watch
for her birthday. In those days the gift of a watch meant the relationship was moving toward an engagement. But she returned the
watch, and one night a few months later, she woke her mother
and told her she was going to marry Dave.

A few months after the wedding, my father was transferred[6]
East. They settled in New York, in the house where I grew up. I
was eight year old when I met my future husband. He was in high
school, a friend of my brother's. I remember him only peripherally[7], as I was much more interested in my brother's other friend —
Francois, a Swiss exchange student, dark, mysterious and pol-
ished.

Fifteen years later the man I would eventually marry came
back to town for Christmas and stopped by my parents' house to
pick up my brother for an evening out. When he saw me in the
next room, he hissed, "Who's that? "

My brother looked at him strangely and said, "It's just Lisa. "
He walked into the room, reintroduced himself and pretended he

我的母亲是那家广播电台的一名撰稿人。他告诉我们说，如果他那天上午不停在分公司，或者他晚两分钟到达那里，那就……我们对这样千载难逢的机会感到既甜蜜又害怕得浑身颤抖，生命——我们的生命——一不留神，就会擦肩而过。

尽管父亲进城时母亲看见过他，但她约会的是别的男人，其中包括一名汽车推销商。在她遇见父亲不久，那位汽车推销商曾送给她一块表作为生日礼物。那个时候，送表作为生日礼物意味着两人的关系正朝着订婚的方向进展。但她将表又还给了那位推销商。几个月后的一天夜里，她摇醒她的母亲，说她要嫁给戴维。

婚礼之后几个月，我的父亲被调到了东部。他们在纽约定居，我就是在纽约的房子里长大的。我8岁那年就遇见了自己的未婚夫。当时他正上高中，他是我的哥哥的一位朋友。我现在只记得他的模糊形象，因为我对我哥哥另一位朋友——弗朗西斯更感兴趣，那是一个瑞士籍交流学生，皮肤黝黑，神秘莫测，体面潇洒。

时隔15年之后，我最终要嫁的那个人回城过圣诞节，碰巧到我的父母家里带我的哥哥晚上一块出去。当他在另一个房

⑤ shiver
/ˈʃɪvə/
v. 颤抖
⑥ transfer
/ˈtrænsˈfɜː/
v. 调动；调任
⑦ peripherally
/pəˈrɪfərəlɪ/
adv. 次要地；边缘地

didn't know how to wrap[8] his Christmas gifts. I pretended to believe him and helped. He came around a lot over the next few
days. "I don't know who's interested in," my mother told me,
"You or your sister." I knew. But later that week I flew across the
country to spend New Year's Eve with another man. Though I'd
been chosen, I wasn't ready to admit it yet.

If the timing had been different, the distance less daunting[9]
and my heart not already albeit[10] unknowingly — engaged, I
could have ended up with that man whom I went off to visit. Or if
not him, then with someone else.

Sometimes I think about that, how time sweeps[11] us along
and puts us in a certain place where we're faced with one option
or another. By chance and by the choices we make, we leave
behind whole other lives we could have lived, full of different pas-
sions and joys, different problems and disappointments.

My father could have missed that picnic. Or my mother could
have picked the car salesman. She would have had other children
and an entirely different future.

Other times — particularly when I come home late to a sleeping house, my husband and daughter curled around each other
after drifting off during the third reading of Jane Yolen's Owl Moon
— I think about the lives we would not have had if chance or
choice had brought us to a different place. And I shiver, much the

间看到我的时候，他故作惊讶地问道：
"这是谁呀？"

我的哥哥莫名其妙地看着他说："是丽莎呀。"他走进房间，重新作了自我介绍，假装不知道怎么包裹他的圣诞礼物。我也假装信以为真，帮了他一把。以后的几天，他又来了好多次。"我不知道他是对谁感兴趣，"母亲告诉我说，"是你还是你的姐姐。"我心明如镜。但后来那个星期，我和另一个男人乘飞机飞越国土去度新年除夕。尽管我已经中选，但我还是不愿意去承认这件事。

如果时间安排不同的话，情况就会大相径庭，再说我的心还没有——尽管心里没底——定下来，我就可以终止跟那个男人外出观光。如果不是他，那就和另外一个人。

有时我就想起那件事，时间是怎么将我们安排到一块，将我们置于某一个地方，我们在那里面对着某种抉择。我们偶尔相遇，就做出了人生的抉择，将我们所过的其它生活统统撇在脑后，充满了截然不同的激情和快乐，遇到了截然不同的问题和失望。

我的父亲也许会错过那次野餐会。或

8 wrap
/ræp/
v. 包或裹

9 daunting
/ˈdɔːntɪŋ/
adj. 吓人的

10 albeit
/ˌɔːlˈbiːɪt/
conj. 虽然；尽管

11 sweep
/swiːp/
v. 带动或移走

way I did as a child at the story of my father's near miss, at the thought that I might have missed this life, this man, this child, this love.

者说，我的母亲可能会选上那个汽车推销商。她会生别的模样的孩子，拥有一个截然不同的未来。

在其它的时间——尤其是当我很晚回家走进沉入梦乡的房间的时候，只见丈夫和女儿在读过第三遍珍妮·约伦的《泉月》渐渐入睡之后相互蜷缩着躺在那里——我想到，如果机会或者选择将我们带到另一个地方，我们就不会来到人世间。尔后，我禁不住浑身颤栗，活像我小时候听父亲讲惊心动魄、九死一生的故事时，或者像在我想到自己也许会错过今生、错过自己的丈夫、错过自己的孩子、错过这次爱情时那样。

Tips for a good night's sleep
晚上睡个好觉的方法

Temperature extremes can make falling asleep difficult or can awaken you from sleep.

温度过高或过低都可能使你难以入睡或从睡梦中醒来。

As a performance benefits from adequate rehearsal[1] and a meal benefits from skilled preparation, a good night's sleep does not just "happen." Sleep experts recommend[2] the following tips to help ensure a good night's sleep. These habits, known to experts as "sleep hygiene[3]," often are sufficient to combat[4] occasional sleep problems. More serious, chronic[5] disorders may require additional techniques. If you have difficulty sleeping night after night or your daytime sleepiness is interfering with your performance at school or work, consult your medical professional or a sleep disorders center. Sleep disorders can be treated successfully.

The National Sleep Foundation recommends the following tips for improving your sleep:

Limit your bedroom use to sleep and sex. Remove the television, desk, computer workstation and other objects that stimulate[6] you, making sleep more difficult. Make your bedroom as pleasant and quiet as possible.

Sleep in a comfortable bed with a comfortable pillow[7]. Find a comfortable sleeping temperature. Temperature extremes[8] can make falling asleep difficult or can awaken you from sleep.

Establish a regular bedtime and bedtime routine and follow them even on weekends. More than an hour's variation from the weekday schedule on the weekend can throw off your biological clock, making Monday morning a particularly difficult time. Avoid bright lights in the evening (which stimulate the body to stay

正像表演得益于充分的排演，一顿饭受益于充分的准备一样，想晚上睡个好觉也不是一下子就能行的。睡眠专家推荐以下几种方法以保证晚上能睡一个好觉。这些习惯，专家们将其作为"睡眠健康"，常常能很好地解决偶然的睡眠问题。更严重的习惯性睡眠失调可能需要更多的解决方法。如果你每晚都不能好好睡觉或因白天想睡觉而干扰了学习或工作，请向医学专家或睡眠失调中心咨询。这样，睡眠失调问题都可以得到很好的解决。

国家睡眠组织推荐下面几种方法用以改善睡眠质量：

卧室的使用仅限于睡觉和性行为。电视、书桌、计算机桌台和其他刺激你的东西都会使你难以入睡，你必须把这些东西搬出卧室。尽可能地使卧室赏心悦目。

睡在一张舒服的床上并配有一个舒服的枕头，调出一个较舒服的睡觉温度。温度过高或过低都可能使你难以入睡或从睡梦中醒来。

设定一个固定的就寝时间和就寝时间规程，每天按照所设定的做，就是在周末也不要违反，如果周末有一个小时以上与平日休息时间不一样的话，就可能使你脱离的生物钟，使得星期一早晨这段时间特别难度过。晚上要避开亮光（光刺激身体而使保持清醒状态），睡觉前试着洗个热水澡，这有助于缓解身体疲劳，降低身体温度，一旦你离开浴盆，一个该睡觉的信号就会传

---

❶ rehearsal
/rɪˈhɜːsl/
n. 排练

❷ recommend
/ˌrekəˈmend/
v. 建议

❸ hygiene
/ˈhaɪdʒiːn/
n. 卫生（学）

❹ combat
/ˈkɒmbæt/
v. 试图减弱或消灭

❺ chronic
/ˈkrɒnɪk/
adj. 长期患病的

❻ stimulate
/ˈstɪmjʊleɪt/
v. 刺激

❼ pillow
/ˈpɪləʊ/
n. 枕头

❽ extreme
/ɪkˈstriːm/
n. 极端不同的状况

awake). Try a warm bath before bedtime. This may help by relaxing the body and by lowering your body temperature once you leave the tub[9] — a signal to the body that it is time to sleep.

Avoid caffeine[10], nicotine[11] and alcohol in the late afternoon and evening. Nicotine and caffeine can delay your sleep and alcohol interferes with your ability to sleep deeply, a key to feeling rested in the morning.

Do not nap[12] during the day if you are having trouble falling asleep at night. The nap may interfere with your ability to fall asleep.

Exercise regularly, 20 to 30 minutes each day if possible, but do it early in the day — at least three hours before going to sleep. Exercise before bed can raise your body temperature — an internal signal to your body to stay awake.

If you cannot fall asleep after 30 minutes, get up and go to another room. Read something entertaining (do not work) or listen to soothing[13] music until you feel sleepy, then return to bed. Use this time to clear your mind, not to try to solve problems that are worrying you.

Let the sunlight help awaken you. Leave curtains open, if possible, or use bright lights when you wake up. The bright light helps the body to reset its biological clock.

到身体里。

　　傍晚和夜间要避开咖啡、烟碱、酒精，烟碱和咖啡会耽搁睡眠时间，酒精会影响睡眠质量，这是早晨觉得困的原因，如果你晚上没睡好觉，白天不要小睡，小睡可能导致晚上不能熟睡。有规律地锻炼，如果可能的话每天锻炼20—30分钟，而且在白天早些时候锻炼——至少在睡觉前3小时。睡觉前锻炼会使身体温度升高——一个使身体清醒的内在信号。

　　如果30分钟后你不能入睡，你要起床走到另外一个房间去，读一些有趣的东西(不要工作)或听令人舒畅的音乐，直到你想睡，然后回到床上去，利用这段时间使头脑清醒，不要试图解决那些一直困扰着你的问题。

　　让太阳光帮助你醒来，当你醒来时，让窗帘敞开着；如果可能的话把亮光利用起来，亮光可以帮助身体重新设定生物钟。

❾ tub

/tʌb/

n. 盆

❿ caffeine

/ˈkæfiːn/

n. 咖啡因

⓫ nicotine

/ˈnɪkətiːn/

n. 尼古丁

⓬ nap

/næp/

n. 小睡

⓭ soothing

/ˈsuːðɪŋ/

adj. 令人舒畅的

The woman in the mirror
镜中的女人

> *Now, all of a sudden, I realized that it was true what people told me, that I was an attractive woman.*

> 现在，我突然意识到人们对我说的话是真的，他们对我说我是一个漂亮的女人。

When I was 11, I found out I had a brain tumor[1]. I had surgery to remove it, but the size and location of the tumor caused my optic[2] nerve to atrophy[3]. For three years afterward, I had partial sight, but my ophthalmologist[4] told me that eventually I would go blind. At the end of my 14th year, doctors pronounced me legally blind and said there was nothing that could be done. I had a 5 percent chance of surviving the tumor, and I did, but somehow I could never deal with the fact that I was going blind. I tried to behave as if everything were just fine. When it happened, I was devastated[5].

My dad left us when I was 5, and I took that really hard. Because of that, and because I was blind on top of it, my greatest fear was that no one was ever going to love me, that I would never get married and have kids and a full life. I was afraid of being alone, and I guess that is what I thought blindness meant.

Ten years later, on Nov. 16 of last year, I was cooking dinner and leaned over to kiss my guide dog, Ami. I lost my balance and hit my head on the corner of my coffee table and then on the floor. It wasn't unusual. When you are blind, you hit yourself all the time. I got up, finished making dinner and went to bed.

When I woke up, I could see. Light was coming through my window, and the curtains were drawn. Of course, I was shocked, but not scared, not like when I lost my sight. There is a big mirror in my bedroom, but I didn't look at myself right away. I wanted to wash my hair and put on make-up[6] first. I do not look good in the

11岁那年,我发现自己得了脑瘤。动手术切除后,肿瘤的大小和位置导致我的视觉神经开始萎缩。那以后的三年里,我还有部分的视力,但是我的眼科医生告诉我,我最终会失明。就在我生命的第14个年头快结束的时候,医生断言我完全失明了,而且没有任何方法可以治疗。患了脑瘤以后,我原本只有5%的机会可以活下来,但是我活下来了。然而,对于我将失明的事实,我却束手无策。我努力使自己表现得好像一切都很好。但是当我真的失明以后,我却一蹶不振了。

我5岁那年父亲就去世了,这对我来说实在是一个难以接受的事实。正因为如此,再加上我失明的缘故,我最大的恐惧就是没有人会爱我,永远都不能结婚,不能有自己的孩子,不能拥有完整的生活。我害怕孤零零的一个人。我想那个时候,这些就是我对失明的理解。

10年过去了。去年11月16日,当时我正在做晚餐。我弯下身子去亲我的导盲犬,它叫阿米(法文"男朋友"的意思)。结果我一下子失去了平衡,头撞在了咖啡桌的一个角上,接着又撞在了地板上。这是很平常的事。一个人要是失明了,总会撞到自己。我爬起来,继续把晚餐做完,然后就上床睡觉了。

当我醒来时,我看见光从窗户透进来,窗

❶ tumor
/ˈtjuːmə/
n. (肿)瘤

❷ optic
/ˈɒptɪk/
adj. 视觉的

❸ atrophy
/ˈætrəfɪ/
n. 萎缩

❹ ophthalmologist
/ˌɒfθælˈmɒlədʒɪst/
n. 眼科医生

❺ devastate
/ˈdevəsteɪt/
v. 令(某人)震惊;使(某人)难以承受

❻ make-up
/ˈmeɪkʌp/
n. 化妆品

morning, and I didn't want to be frightened. As I was showering, I caught my reflection[7]. And just that left me speechless, really.

The last time I saw myself, I had short hair, a pale complexion[8] and features that didn't show because I had such light eyebrows[9] and eyelashes[10]. I looked awful, like a teenage girl, I suppose. Now, all of a sudden, I realized that it was true what people told me, that I was an attractive woman. When I stood in front of the mirror, I reached to touch my face. That is what I had been doing for 10 years — it was how I understood — so it was a natural impulse[11]. It was not until I saw myself that I realized how much my memory had faded[12] of things I once could see. It was about four hours before I told anyone. I stayed with Ami. We looked at each other and played outside in the yard. I just wanted to be alone, and take it in. It was so much.

The strange thing was that I knew it was going to happen. About a week before, I was walking Ami and suddenly saw blue dots in front of my left eye, the one I would regain my sight in. I told my mum because I found it funny; blue had been my favorite color and was the easiest color for me to see when I had partial sight. I took it as a sign.

People don't treat me differently now. I was always completely independent. I lived in Auckland, New Zealand, in my own -flat with my dog. I would have parties and go clubbing. I would listen to the beat of the music and go with it and hope for the best. When your friends grab you and point you in the other direction

帘是拉上的。当然,我吃了一惊,但没有像我失明的时候那样感到害怕。我的卧室里有一面大镜子,但是我并没有马上去看自己的模样。我想先洗洗头,画上妆。早晨我的样子总是不好看,我不想吓着自己。沐浴的时候,我看见了自己的影子,我顿时说不出话来,真的。

　　我最后一次看见自己的时候,我留着短发,脸色苍白,而且面容黯淡,那是因为我的眉毛和睫毛都很稀少。我想自己那时候很难看,就像一个十几岁的小女孩。现在,我突然意识到人们对我说的话是真的,他们对我说我是一个漂亮的女人。我站在镜子面前,伸出手去触摸自己的脸。我这样做有10年了——我当时是这么理解的——所以这是一种自然的冲动。直到我看见自己,我才意识到自己曾经能看见的东西都已经在很大程度上从我的记忆中消退了。4个小时以后,我才将我复明的事情告诉别人。我和阿米在一起,我们互相看着对方,在外面的院子里玩耍。我只想独自一人接受这一事实,因为对我来说这实在是意义重大。

　　奇怪的是,在这之前,我就知道我会复明。大概一个星期前,我牵着阿米去散步,突然看见我的左眼前面有蓝色的点。左眼就是我后来复明的那只眼睛。我觉得很有趣,于是告诉了妈妈。蓝色一直是我最喜欢的颜色,也是在我

❼ reflection
/rɪˈflekʃn/
n. 映像;影子

❽ complexion
/kəmˈplekʃn/
n. 面色,脸色

❾ eyebrow
/ˈaɪbraʊ/
n. 眉毛

❿ eyelash
/ˈaɪlæʃ/
n. 睫毛

⓫ impulse
/ˈɪmpʌls/
n. 突如其来的念头;冲动

⓬ fade
/feɪd/
v. 逐渐消失,变得模糊不清

because they are actually over there， that is when you remember you're blind.

I also loved movies. Going to the movies blind was like someone telling you a really good story with great sound effects， and you make up all the images in your head. I haven't been back since I regained my sight. But I've been able to see my favorite soap， "Shortland Street." And my friends took out magazines and pointed out Pamela Lee Anderson and Brad Pitt. The biggest surprise was Brad Pitt. I just thought， What is everyone going on about? The best was seeing my boyfriend. He rode the ferry[13] over， and I knew him the moment I saw him. He was as sexy as I had imagined.

I am not surprised that things are pretty much the same in my life. I didn't expect anything more than what I have now. I worked very hard to surround myself with genuine people and to create a normal life for myself. I am still the same person： It just means that physically， perhaps， I can share more and put the two together： the feelings I had， with sight.

The same doctor who told me I would never see again told me I had regained 80 percent of the vision in my left eye. To be able to look him in the eye and tell him I could see again -- honestly， that felt pretty damn good. He ran all the tests and made me read the eye chart[14], but he has no explanation. He said himself， and still says， that once the optic nerve is damaged, it cannot regenerate.

只有部分视力的时候最容易看清的颜色。我把这当作是我复明的一个信号。

现在，人们不再以不同的方式对待我了。我一直都是一个完全独立的人。我住在新西兰的奥克兰市，和我的狗住在我自己的公寓里。我经常参加各种聚会和俱乐部的活动。我也会听着音乐，和着它的节拍，希望最好的事情会发生。只有当你的朋友一把抓住你，指着另一个方向，告诉你他们实际上在那边的时候，你才想起来自己看不见。

我也很喜欢看电影。对于一个失明的人来说，去看电影就好像有人在给你讲一个好故事，伴着精彩的音响效果，你可以在脑海中想象出各种形象。我复明之后还没有去看过电影。但是我一直在看我最喜欢的肥皂剧，"苏特兰街"。我的朋友们拿出杂志，把帕梅拉·李·安德森和布拉德·皮特指给我看。最让我吃惊的是布拉德·皮特。我只是在想，他有什么让人喜欢的呢？最美好的事情是看见了我的男朋友。他是坐渡船过来的，我第一眼看见他的时候就认出他是我的男朋友。他和我想象中的一样性感。

生活中的一切都和以前一样，对此我一点儿也不感到惊讶。我从来没有期望能得到更多的东西。我努力地工作，好让自己置身于真诚

❸ **ferry**
/ˈferɪ/
n. 渡船
❹ **chart**
/tʃɑːt/ *n.* 图或表

I don't think the knock on the head had anything to do with it. If others want to believe that is how it happened, that is fine. But I consider this a miracle. There is no other way to describe it. Some things just cannot be explained. Of course, some people are skeptical[15]. For me, it is precious. I try not to think about the possibility of going blind again. But my recovery would be no less a miracle even if I lost my sight tomorrow.

的人们中间,给自己创造正常的生活。我还是我:复明对于我来说,也许只是意味着生理上能分享更多的东西, 还有, 能将两者放在一起——过去的感受和重见的光明。

　　那个以前说我再也不能复明的医生告诉我说,我的左眼视力已经恢复了80%。我能看着他的眼睛,告诉他我又能看见了,老实说,这感觉实在是太好了。他给我做了各种测试,让我读视力检查表,但是他没有作任何的解释。他自己以前说过,现在还在这么说,视觉神经一旦被破坏是不能再生的。

　　我并不认为我那天撞到了头和我的复明有任何关系。如果别人要认为有关系,那也可以。但是我认为这是一个奇迹。再没有别的方式来描述这件事了。有些事情是解释不通的。当然,有人会对此表示怀疑。可对我来说,它是十分宝贵的。我努力不去想重新失明的可能性。但是,就算我明天就会失明,我的视力的恢复也仍是一个奇迹。

⑮ skeptical
/ˈskeptɪkl/
adj. 常怀疑的

图书在版编目（CIP）数据

英汉对照·心灵阅读. 2，生活篇/张斌彦，董新颖编译. —北京：外文出版社，2004
ISBN 7 – 119 – 03744 – 7

Ⅰ. 英… Ⅱ.①张… ②董… Ⅲ. 英语 – 对照读物 – 英、汉 Ⅳ. H319.4

中国版本图书馆 CIP 数据核字（2004）第 058988 号

外文出版社网址：
　http://www.flp.com.cn
外文出版社电子信箱：
　info@flp.com.cn
　sales@flp.com.cn

英汉对照·心灵阅读（二）

生　活　篇

编　译　张斌彦　董新颖
审　校　林　立

责任编辑　王　蕊　相　永
封面设计　时振晓
印刷监制　张国祥
出版发行　外文出版社
社　　址　北京市百万庄大街 24 号　　邮政编码　100037
电　　话　（010）68995963/6075（编辑部）
　　　　　（010）68329514/68327211（推广发行部）
印　　刷　北京中印联印务有限公司
经　　销　新华书店/外文书店
开　　本　大 32 开　　　　　　字　　数　150 千字
印　　数　10001 – 15000 册　　印　　张　8.375
版　　次　2005 年 6 月第 1 版第 2 次印刷
装　　别　平
书　　号　ISBN 7 – 119 – 03744 – 7/H · 1628（外）
定　　价　15.80 元